Creating Business Beyond this Reality

Happy Publishing

ISBN 978-0-9983708-9-7

A special thanks and acknowledgment to the tools of Access Consciousness® as mentioned in some of the following chapters by individual authors. Please go to www.AccessConsciousness.com for more information.

Published by Happy Publishing, www.HappyPublishing.net

Table of Contents

When You Don't Fit In, Create Something New

I wasn't raised to own a business. I was born into a family of writers and television producers, publishers and printers. I was praised when I wrote poems and songs, and I was praised when my poems were published.

The creative spark I've always known as my reality was nurtured and coveted in my house. It was welcomed to be a dreamer and to be relatively out of touch with reality.

I was magic from early on, and I could speak telepathically with animals, babies, anyone and anything. I could chat with people in their 30s when I was 11 or 12, and have conversations they would remember.

The pain of the neglect of the business and financial components of my upbringing became apparent in high school, when my family didn't buy me anything that the other children had. This got worse in college, when I was given an ultimatum to go to a top university but then left there to "fund" it myself. I was 17, living on my own, and as Maya Angelou's poem says, "Still I Rise."

I started working as a waitress, and then just adding jobs until I could pay for my stark lifestyle. Then, I chose writing. The breaks

1

into being paid to write came quickly. I wrote for the college newspaper and college magazines. I could write well enough to be paid to write anywhere I chose to live. This landed me in Santa Barbara, writing for the Santa Barbara daily newspaper. What a beautiful place to be!

When I look back at the very little I was shown or taught about business, it's not surprising I ran into major obstacles when running my own business. Even though I could write, and even though I understood the publishing business, I didn't understand the business of publishing. Then I began to ask more questions, and communicate with the energy of my business.

I am still being paid to write and edit, and now I can live anywhere in the world. I added publishing and podcasting to the mix. It seems that the three books grew to 50 titles relatively quickly, and Happy Publishing was born.

The company has a fast and wild spirit. When this book showed up for me to create (I get ideas and then they turn into books), I was hungry for the knowledge the authors would provide.

I have grown so much over the creation of this book. I learned about business, and a lot about creativity. When I ask for more, more happens. When I began to speak to my business, I saw this eager, expansive, ambitious, kind, compassionate, imperfect, and expressive entity. It was for me to build as an alternative, a company that I wished had existed when I first became a published author.

I looked to create beyond the current reality, and I invited brilliant beings of light to join me on this journey.

On the following pages, you will meet some of the most intelligent, creative, powerful and wonderful beings on the planet today. I invite you to a new way of being with business, where joy is present, and creativity abounds.

Erica Glessing
CEO, Happy Publishing

CHAPTER 1

Monetize Your Creativity the You-way

KATARINA NILSSON

There's only one you, but who says you must be only one thing? When you allow more of what's really you into your life and business, you will gain from it in ways you never imagined. Creation comes in all kinds of different shapes, but when it knocks on your door, make sure to embrace it and let it take you on new adventures. I did, and from that moment I've never looked back. Until today, that is, since my personal story actually suits the topic of this little piece and symbolizes the true meaning of monetizing your creativity.

No luck and all stuck. But I found magic in a brush!

So let's back the tape a few years, to a time I feel strangely distant from today, but also one that I've learnt a lot from. After a couple of hectic years as a young and ambitious talent in the naming industry, trying to deal with all my clients and living after other people's expectations and projections of me became too much. I just ran over myself and hit the wall big time.

In reality, I loved working with name creation for big companies and products, but I still felt a sort of void in my business, one that didn't necessarily have anything to do with all my personal drama. To reload and start anew, I found what became the most relaxing thing in the world for me — painting. In the most positive sense, I became totally obsessed with acrylic creations! And would you know it, before I even realized it I had enough material for a whole exhibition. But come on, naming was my profession, I was hardly a REAL artist. Or was I?

Some of the biggest barriers in most people's lives are the fear of being judged and not being good enough. To create in your own bubble is one thing, but to showcase your creations to the world? Yes, it takes some gut, but few things beat the feeling of crushing that chain of self-doubt. So what the hell, I thought, and went for it. I decided to host an art show of my own. Exciting indeed!

The exhibition took place in central Stockholm, Sweden, and was an instant success. Not only did people show up, they actually liked what they saw and bought the paintings! I couldn't have imagined such a reception in my wildest dreams but for me the big win was that giant leap from thought to action. However, I also realized that painting really could be more than just a hobby, so why not make my greatest passion a natural part of my everyday business?

We all know that we should do more of what we love, and still so few of us make it a reality. Now that my artwork is highly integrated in my business life, I can't even explain why I hesitated to begin with. I guess sometimes what's that light and easy for you is hard to see as a business.

"Why don't we just do more of what we love? If we feel no joy in what we create, then why do we even bother doing it?"

When you let more creativity into your life and business, it has instant impact and just keeps delivering. From here on, I will talk more about how to use the creative power within you to create and explore further.

Work hard, play hard. Or simply create with ease?

When people are asked if they desire more wealth and money in life, the majority will obviously answer yes. But if you take a closer look at common points of view around money, you will see that it's actually not the case at all. Sure, they want the sweet dollars, but very often people aren't willing to do what it takes to get there. The fact is that if you want to receive you have to ask for it, and many times the unwritten rules and limitations around money stop you from doing that. By learning how to erase these obstacles and letting more joy and creation come into your life and business, chances are you will also become a real money magnet.

So how do you actually achieve this?

The first step is to start asking yourself questions, such as: What are my points of view on money and are they really mine? Most people have prejudices about money and what it means to be poor, wealthy or something in between. The environment in which we live and work has a very strong influence on the way we look at things, and if you choose another direction people will judge you for it.

This judgment of others — from friends, family and colleagues to people on social media you don't even really know — is challenging not to get affected by. But if you desire a different financial reality it's necessary to create what you really desire. *Buy this car. Vote for this guy. Your hair looks better that way.* People will aways tell you what to do and how to act, but remember that your business — and your life — is no one else's business. Why have their will as your own?

For me it was about embracing art, for you it might be something completely different. It doesn't matter what you create, only that you create. A very good place to start, is to be grateful for what you've already created so far and acknowledge your creative power. Judgment is never a boost for creativity, it's actually quite the opposite. Instead of judging your creations, ask yourself where you can take it from here and what else you can choose. There's always a new adventure waiting if you're ready to choose and receive it. Keep in mind that money follows joy!

So how do you know what is your own point of view?

What's true for you always makes you feel lighter. If the way you create and look at things gives you a sense of heaviness in your body, it's not true for you. When you're aware of what's holding you back, you no longer have to buy in to the points of view of others. Always follow what you know, and the road ahead will open for possibilities you haven't had before.

To start creating with ease, you can ask yourself the following questions:

1. Do I follow my head or my gut?

A majority of our best decisions actually come from our gut. It's wise to be wise, but at the same time, our thoughts can be deceiving. Many times they aren't even our own, our points of view belong to someone else. Our points of view create our reality, so always trust what you *know* is right for you.

2. What's so fun for me that I would do it even if it gave me zero cents?

If you know the answer — start using that something in your business! People always say you shouldn't mix business with pleasure. There's a very accurate reply to that statement: why?

When we choose more of what we love to do it usually affects all aspects of life, including business.

3. Do I focus on problems or possibilities?

If you desire to increase the ease, stop limiting yourself in your business. The more you focus your energy on the perceived problems in life, the more it will limit your creation. So when possibility knocks — embrace the adventure and see where it leads you!

4.   Am I me with money?

Few things are as powerful as the projection of others. Inspiration is one thing, but to have someone else's will as your own is a big pitfall when it comes to creation. Our views on money are very often inherited by our family, friends and society. So make sure your views on creativity and business are your own. When you're truly being you with money, what can you choose and create? Are you aware that you create your own financial reality from the creative choices you make?

> "It doesn't matter what you create,
> only that you create"

Creation from relaxation – how to really get things done with ease

Now you may be thinking: *Creating with ease is easier said than done.* Well, change looks different from person to person, but my take is that it's never easier to be stuck in the hard way of doing things. Of that I am a living example. With the right tools and know-how, you will see how creation from relaxation is so much more rewarding.

Some jobs require an intense level of creativity. The task at hand demands you to be constantly on the edge and innovative. Although some people enjoy that sort of pressure, it's probably more common that it chokes rather than empowers creation. For many of us, our best ideas appear out of nowhere when we don't even try. This can actually be implemented to how you create in your business.

> "Why let creation become a burden, when it's supposed to be joyful?"

When we're in a state of relaxation, it's so much easier to gain access to our creativity and get into the "zone". And with a greater sense of creativity comes progress, both when it comes to our souls and our sales. It may sound completely obvious, but if so — how come so many of us still build our existence around the expectations of others? If people agree that creation should be freed from the chains of demands, why don't we all just practice what we preach?

I believe that creativity should never be dragged out of you. Think about some of the greatest ideas and creations known to man, like Isaac Newton and his law of gravity. When he had his famous *aha*-moment, one that actually changed the world, no one held a gun to his head. He was, however, hit in the head by an apple. Rewarding creativity always seems to work in that way. *"The sculpture just came to me." "The song seemingly wrote itself"*. Many historic masterpieces have been made when the creator has been in a place of total ease and relaxation — the space of receiving.

So how do you get to that magical creative state of mind? For starters, you need to open your mind to what a creation actually is, because really, it could be anything.

Let me give you a little example. In my studio where I create my paintings, I usually keep a smaller canvas on the side. I use it to wipe off spare colour and never pay much attention to it. At several occasions, the spare canvas has ended up more interesting to me than the real piece I've been working on, that is harder to free from expectations. This is no coincidence — when you're at ease, creation comes to you from places you least would have guessed. No matter if it's a splash of paint or an apple falling from a tree.

Stop chasing creativity. Simply relax and let it come to you instead! By being willing to receive it, you will benefit your soul as much as your sales. Remember:

1. Creation loves an open mind

Other people will always put expectations and judgments on you. When you no longer let that affect you, the pressure you've put on yourself will disolve and you can create more freely.

2. You and your creations are different things

When people judge your creations, it has nothing to do with who you are as a person. Keep following what you know is true for you, not for anyone else. Your value actually has nothing to do with the value of your painting, song, performance piece or audition tape. Once you are able to distance yourself from your creations, it will also be so much easier to let go and sell them. Creation is about learning, but that doesn't exclude it can also be about earning.

3. Go create, never hesitate!

The more you create the more inspired you will be. Don't overthink it, just take action and more creation will appear out of the blue!

"Creation from relaxation benefits both your soul and your sales"

Create to Make Money to Create

So what's money even got to do with creativity? Isn't being creative reward enough?

Don't get me wrong — finding the key to your inner world where creation flows freely is an amazing experience. What I want each and everyone to do is to find the means to make the most of it. Since the beginning of time, we've been force-fed the same old notion that money is ugly and shouldn't be allowed near "fine art". If that's how you feel, ok. But here's the twist: What if money could be seen from a new point of view, as a tool to further explore and create? What if you and your creations are a great gift to the world?

No matter if you create on a big arena or in your garage, people will still judge what you do and have their fixed opinions on this and that. Therefore, you won't really do yourself any favors if you choose the *starving-but-true-artist-route*. Once again, that's all about the fear of the judgment of others — it's *damned if you do, damned if you don't*. So if you ask me: do! Just get going and monetize your creativity.

"Money can be used to explore and take your creativity to places unknown."

Although I'm all for creation done with total ease, I don't think it's necessarily the most rewarding thing to feel safe in the things you create at all times. Because the truth is — too comfortable is not too creative. Many times, the greatest satisfaction comes from entering deep waters. These waters or places unknown are yours to discover and if someone tells you you're out of your depth, that's actually a good indication that you're on to something truly special!

Creation is never about what other people expect. It's about searching, listening to yourself and keep looking forward — never sideways where the jealous are lined up to judge you or backwards where only what's already done exists.

You can always come up with excuses for not taking creativity to the next level, but those excuses will only limit creation and leads to absolutely nothing but regret. People who make a statement about how art must be separated from money at all cost (no pun intended) are often the ones who are simply too afraid to step out of their own box and see how far they can take it. Why waste your time on creating limitations, when you could be creating possibilities instead?

The trick is to shut out all judgement and negativity and follow your creative instincts without thinking about possible reactions. No matter what you create it can never please everyone so just leave that impossible desire out of the equation. Instead, explore new ways and play around with your creativity.

Choosing different, to constantly see what else is possible, surely makes things exciting and interesting. It's also rewarding. What I would love for you to do, is to start seeing money as a direct investment in your creativity. Give yourself the possibility of greatness on your own terms and it will affect every part of your life!

Let me wrap things up by giving you a few final thoughts, tips and tools to start monetizing your creativity:

1.   There is no competition

We never believe we're good enough, that's the curse of mankind. I'm here to tell you that *you are*. When it comes to expressing yourself, there are no written rules, only your rules. What others do is not your business and what you do is no one else's business. So remember: what you create can never be wrong, and actually, if people tell you it is you're probably on the right track!

2.   Let's turn up the weird!

Honestly, how much fun is it to always play it safe? Looking outside of the box, on the other hand, is often very inspiring. If you decide to make a creative change, go all in and let your creation take you to new unexpected dimensions.

3.   Be the u in unique

The world hardly needs a copy of something we've seen a million times before. What the world really desires is you. When you express more of what's really you without taking the demands of anyone or anything into consideration, your creation will find its true place. Remember, there's a chair for every ass — someone will always find your art totally amazing! But the most important thing is that you do and that you have fun with it.

4.   Always out-create yourself

Keep asking yourself these questions:

What can I be and do to out-create myself today? Is there something I would like to do that I haven't tried before? What else is possible? What will it create if I do it this way instead? Go with what's light and have fun with the things that come your way.

5.   The comfort zone is a no-go zone

If you're on your way out of the fear-box or if you've already found the creative flow — amazing! Now is not the time to stop going. Sustainable growth comes from constantly making new choices and never stop, wait or hesitate. That's what creating with ease and joy actually means and the more you do it, the more expansive it gets!

I always tell people to go f-ing create! I did it my way. What's yours?

The Author

Katarina Nilsson

www.CreatingBusinessBeyondThisReality.com/katarina-nilsson

CHAPTER 2

Be Your Business: Everything is Possible!

Tina Devine

Two suitcases... That's what my life has reduced to. The space from the last 10 years now feels empty and insignificant. What the fuck have I done? Did I really need to sell everything I own?

Deep breath... you asked for this. No, you demanded this!! When you really ask for change and demand different, the universe provides. Always!

What does this have to do with creating business beyond this reality I hear you ask... EVERYTHING!! Let me explain...

My name is Tina Devine (yup that's my real name) and before you and I found each other here, I was a career-driven woman in business for over 20 years. I had only one perspective on how to create business and that was to WORK. The more hours I worked, the more I justified the need and desire to do more. The results from this approach varied from huge success and elation to almost bankruptcy and devastation as well as having a huge impact on my personal relationships and health. There's only so much multi-tasking you can do, right?

I thought that if I stayed strong, focused and positive it would be enough. But it was never enough... I was never enough...

Many of my business ventures amounted to huge superficial wins that left me feeling empty. Everything I reached for was on the outside, and what I really needed was to do the inner work. Basically, I learned to give till I couldn't give any more.

What I got in return was resentment with a side of completely losing my identity in everyone around me. Does any of this sound familiar? It wasn't pretty feeling blinded and exhausted by my life. It's a story that trapped me until I finally hit bottom... and from this space of desperation I started to ask the question, what else is possible?

When you ask questions, the answers can show up in many ways. Mine started with my own version of eat pray love. I left my husband, my home and my business and ran away to Sri Lanka and found sanctuary in a yoga and Ayurveda retreat. * I am by no means suggesting you take such radical action to create space, I just want to share the catalyst of events that occurred.

Little did I know my breakdown would become a permission slip to breakthrough... more of that later.

During this time, I had many epiphanies ... and the saying "when the student is ready the teacher appears", could not have been truer for me. Messengers and synchronicities came to me from the strangest of places and because I was asking from a place of desperation, I had no choice but to surrender. Little did I know this would create the space I needed to receive and finally listen.

And that's how I changed the impossible into I'm possible?

My perspective on how I show up in my life and business changed. For the first time, I realized that I didn't need to DO more, I needed to BE more.

Fast forward two years and both my story and reality are so very different.

Imagine... Waking up to the sound of the waves in the Caribbean. After a one day visit on a cruise you enjoy the energy and feel of the place so much that 2 weeks later you move there. Just because you can! The beach is at your door and every morning, the sun's warmth excites and energizes you as you take your gratitude walk to the coffee shop. There is no work schedule that must be done, only that which feels playful, fun and inspired. Creative ideas flow effortlessly as do clients and opportunities and life feels spacious, exciting and full of possibilities.

This is not a dream, or wishful thinking. This is my current reality and every day I pinch myself and feel so full of gratitude and appreciation. How did I get so lucky? How did I create this reality? How does it get better than this? (Because I know it can and it will)

So how did I make such a huge change in my reality? It didn't happen overnight, but I had recognized that I needed to do different. It started with reiki and the exploration of energy and the more space I created for me, the better I felt and the more I immersed myself in further teachings.

I learnt that everything is energy vibrating at different frequencies, from thoughts to things, and we all have the power to create exactly what we want. Being the control freak Virgo, this resonated perfectly (although I have since learnt the power of allowing and letting go), and each of my desires began to manifest effortlessly.

> "If you want to find the secrets of the universe, think in terms of energy, frequency and vibration."
> ~ Nikola Tesla

Being a woman on the other side of those feelings of being defeated by my life and business, here's what I want to share with you. Embracing change is your fastest way to correcting your course to your true desires. Perception is everything and we get to be the author of our life, because we choose what we believe every moment of every day.

What happens in our mind and heart is directly reflected and actively creates the world around us. I know, it's deep. But once you recognize everything is vibrational, you will tap into your emotions and take back control of your internal guidance system and start truly shaping the world around you.

What does this mean in practical terms for you? How can you start to create the changes you want to BE?

What if you asked yourself the following questions? Am I ready for growth and change? Am I willing to make a commitment to me? Am I prepared to implement new daily habits that will create space for the energy and changes I desire? Are you nodding yet?

I walk my talk with this. Without implementing some simple practices every day, I would have no emotional guidance system to deliberately create the life I want. My life would quickly spin back out of control and I would be reacting out of fear instead of love.

Here's what I've learned over the years, it doesn't matter how many books you read. Thought without engagement will leave you in the same place you started.

This system saved my life and my sanity. I call it Manifesting for the modern woman because it's fast and flexible and will impact your life in as little as 15 minutes a day.

As busy women in business, we perhaps don't have time to spend hours meditating, writing affirmations, visualizing or journaling. All of which are fantastic tools by the way, but which one produces results for you? Our reality is represented by our senses and we each have a dominant way that we receive and give meaning to our experiences. Are you visual, auditory or kinesthetic?

The fastest way to manifesting is recognizing your hot spots and blind spots, in terms of how you receive and process information or energy and then you can focus on the specific tools that work fast for you. To help you find out your manifesting archetype, I have created a free quiz and information download of the tools designed just for you (www.tina-devine/quiz)

"I think; therefore, I Am..."

I start my day, every day with these two little words I AM.

At the start of the chapter I talked about demanding change. These two small words are the most powerful magic making tools you could ever use. Its more than just an affirmation. When you make any statement starting with I Am... it becomes a declaration, a demand on the universe for what you really want.

I AM... is of the highest frequency, and speaking, thinking, feeling or writing it down (depending on your hot spot) generates the energy and vibrations to create change so that you shift your internal experience to create a world that serves you.

Using this simple formula will make it easy for you to remember and incorporate a daily practice that will strengthen your manifesting muscle to become a deliberate creator of the type of business and life you dream of... the key word being deliberate.

I	=	Intention with Imagination
A	=	Amplify with Appreciation, Align, (inspired) Action & Allow
M	=	Momentum to Manifest

It starts with intention to give your day direction. The energy behind intention is faster than the speed of light. Have you ever experienced thinking about someone and then they call you, or ever wondered why some of your connections on Social media respond to your posts at the exact time you send it? Your intention is so powerful it already starts the creation process from your thoughts before you take any other actions.

This realization was a game changer for me.

The science bit: So, this is where imagination comes in to play. Your brain cannot distinguish between past, present of future, real or imagined and will create neural pathways or circuits from your dominant thoughts before reflecting them into your reality. By setting powerful I AM intentions and amplifying the energy with imagination, emotion and questions you can redesign your reality. Nuts, right?

However, it's not enough to just think happy thoughts, although that is a perfect first step... you still must do, but the difference is to take inspired actions. What does that mean? It means giving yourself space to receive, whether that's in meditation, in having delicious me-time or creating a business that is your playground where fun is the energy that drives results. When you want different, you must do different or rather I should say BE different.

This, I have to admit, was the hardest adjustment for me. Even though I was seeing amazing results in both my life and business, old beliefs of you should work hard for your money and you're having too much time travelling and having fun, brought up emotions of judgement and guilt (for not doing more) or triggers of business shouldn't be this easy. So, if old wounds appear in the process know that this is very normal but also recognize they no longer need to be accepted as part of your new normal!

Inspired actions come in many formats. It might be an awareness to call someone, or a desire to take a different route when out walking. (You know those out of the blue moments!) Trust in the impulses you receive and watch the magic unfold. You can amplify the energy around any desire with appreciation and gratitude for where you are now and the excitement for where you want to BE. The universal law of attraction will always respond to your vibration which means you always attract more of what you BE.

This may be the most difficult concept to overcome. When your business is out of control and you're desperate to change, how do you feel appreciation and gratitude for where you are at? Contrast is the unsung hero in creation. You did just read that correctly. It's the contrast which causes us to ask for more, to launch desires. BUT... you need to find the wisdom in your wounds, the gratitude for the lessons, the appreciation for the change it creates. It starts with taking responsibility and soothing and removing self-judgment as you reach for slightly better thoughts to raise your vibration to attract better. There is always another perspective.

My favorite technique is the gratitude walk. Every morning I walk along the beach and start from A-Z of what I am grateful for. By H I'm smiling, by S I'm giggling (hmm I wonder which s comes to mind) and by Z I'm ready for anything... zebras will do that every time!

Your intentions plus high vibrational energy will always create momentum as one inspired action leads effortlessly to another. It's what is often described as being in the flow or the zone and it's the space of creation where manifestation follows.

Below are case studies of two amazing women that I was honored to work with to implement powerful changes:

Amber, a successful business director, mother of a small child and wife, from the outside had the perfect life. But internally she was struggling with guilt that if she was working hard her family would suffer and vice versa. Her desire to up level in work was tainted with the belief that to do so would mean doing more when she was already stretched, with no time or space for herself.

Within 3 months of working together, a combination of allowing new perspectives and implementing the daily practice of journaling and gratitude, Amber saw huge shifts and changes to her reality.

In her words...

"What Tina teaches isn't textbook, it's not counselling, it's deeper than that. You learn about yourself and how fantastic you already are. You learn to love the insignificant by learning that's the most significant! Tina taught me to love myself and in turn, receive love.

I am powerful, I am strong and most of all I am. That's it. I am. I can make who I am whatever I want to be, I just need to think it, believe it and then live it.

Twelve months ago I was unhappy. Correction, I thought I was unhappy. I wasn't, I just didn't feel like I was living as the best version of me and I had lost the belief in myself. Now, in just a year, I have my dream home, a new business, a fantastic relationship with my husband, a good (ever working) relationship with money and my guilt is going. It is not gone. I have good days and I have down days. The thing is now, I embrace the down days as they allow me time to reflect, to rebalance and refocus. If there is resistance, I know now that I have the power to change it.

Thanks to Tina I have found my inner strength again and I am back in the game. Loving it".

Amber, Director, UK

Lana is a life mastery expert, online course creator and entrepreneur at www.lanashlafer.com. She runs a thriving multiple 6-figure business and is also a wife and mother of 3. During the last 6 months Lana has unlevelled in so many ways: from moving into a dream mansion, tripling her business income and growing her team to allow more ease and support.

There were times when this elevation felt challenging and difficult. Together we visualized and created a new landscape, one with a deeper foundation and stronger walls to allow a new level of support and growth. A place with more space for Lana to BE more and let go of the Doing. A reality where being out of control is not only allowed but encouraged. A place of trust and deep surrender.

The result is that not only did Lana reach more people in her programs and saw more positive impact in the world with her work, but she felt more playful, easeful and free in her life!

"Tina is such a wonderful visionary partner to imagine a new reality with more effortless abundance, more creativity and play and more amazing people to support me every step of the way. And the things that we imagined and discussed manifested so quickly! So glad I have her wisdom and insight as I up level and grow!"

Lana Shlafer, CEO, California

Home play:

Let's take this theory into play. Get a piece of paper and write down 10 I AM ... statements relevant to your core desires and changes you want to create in your new business reality

It's important to highlight here the power of your words and thoughts so the key is to use words that feel fully aligned with your desires. For example, although one of my core desires was to incorporate more travel, when I used the statement I am free it did not resonate as my belief at that time was that freedom as I perceived it wasn't possible and so the energy behind the statement for me was in fact that I am trapped. A better choice for me was I Am a traveler, or I Am a location independent entrepreneur.

Now look at your list and on a scale of 1-10 with 10 being the highest give each statement a score based on your current beliefs of what is possible. Repeat the declarations and feel into your awareness. Does your body feel light or heavy? Remove any statements that feel heavy and score under 8 and reword them until they feel powerful, achievable and exciting.

Now you have your sweet spots to focus on... It only needs a few minutes a day to allow your imagination to expand and feel into the energy of the words. Use your hot spot tools and let the creation and fun begin.

Everything that you have lived provides a great roadmap for where you want to go. There is never a final destination as we continue to experience, contract, ask and expand. This makes it more vital to love the process of becoming and enjoy every step of the journey.

Your business, like you, will evolve through the stages of I am, I can, I will, I do to finally I BE. This is how everything is created from thought to action to becoming. But, it is never about the how!! And it's not about what you know. It's about showing up... Every day and choosing to say YES to you.

There are many ways to Be your business beyond this reality and here are a few of my favourites that have helped to keep me focused excited and aligned with my desires.

Be Passion: Your business is an extension of you. What lights you up and gets you giddy with excitement? What are you really good at? What comes so naturally to you that you almost take it for granted and don't recognise it as your biggest asset or skill? That's who you BE. Make that your business and see how effortlessly your energy of excitement gathers momentum and growth. Everything else within your business should be outsourced to allow you to focus on your zone of genius and the areas that bring you joy. It should never be hard!

Be the question: Keep asking questions of what else is possible? What do you need to change? What's the best choice to make in this moment? Trust your emotions and intuition to guide you with a focus on what makes you feel good. Your business is you and you are here to feel delight and satisfaction in all you do. And even when it feels amazing keep asking how does it get better than this? Allow the possibilities you haven't yet considered to become available to you.

Be comfort: You've heard the saying it's time to step out of your comfort zone, right? Wrong? Words hold energy and intent. It would be more accurate to say get out of your uncomfortable zone. That's the place where sadly a lot of people live feeling unsupported, unfulfilled, lacking purpose and clarity and completely shut off from recognizing and honoring their own needs.

I know because I was one of those people!

So now it no longer makes sense for me to say I need to be uncomfortable to grow. How about a new perspective to your Comfort zone as a place of possibilities where you can be you? A place where you can stretch and expand in comfort with the necessary knowledge and systems. A place where you can feel nurtured and integrate at your own speed following your core desires. A place where the foundation will grow deeper and wider to support your growth and where there are no ceilings or limits to what you can achieve. A place where you are so fired up following your passions that you can't stop the momentum of miracles that constantly show up for you. Oh yes!! Let's get more comfy.

Be wealth: Love yourself to wealth! Wealth is an energy and one that women in particular, have tied up with their beliefs around working hard, earning it and self-worth. It's about serving and being a contribution in all that you do but also allowing yourself to receive, whether that's a compliment, a free coffee, offered support from friends and partners or a million-dollar contract. The success of your business and balance of your bank account are inextricably linked to your beliefs around what you feel you deserve and you cannot fully give when you do not allow yourself to receive. So, start saying yes because you are worth it

What's next? The evolution of you and your business...

How does it get better than this? How do you keep creating beyond your current reality? Beyond that which you can perceive or even imagine? This is the other side of imagination and is the space of infinite possibilities. To access this next level of consciousness just remember to always BE the question, BE in your comfort zone, BE your business, and BE unstoppable... because you are!

The Author

Tina Devine
www.CreatingBusinessBeyondThisReality.com/tina-devine

CHAPTER 3

Creating a Business that Works for You

Kass Thomas

What is your brand of magic?

The idea of creating a business of my own has always appealed to me.

I know it can be a lot of hard work, long hours and determination.

My mom had her own business. My dad was a dedicated worker. In fact, I come from a hard-working family and being committed to my job and my work is something that was instilled in me from a young age.

I myself started working when I was 14, selling ice cream on an ice cream truck and have worked in a variety of jobs and fields continuously all of my life.

So, I'm no stranger to working 20 hours a day, rolling up my sleeves and getting the job done, even in the face of obstacles. Where others might choose to go home early, throw in the towel, doubt, or get fed up, I have always been willing to bring the project to completion, even if it meant doing it all by myself.

Great qualities to have: dedication, perseverance, and a 'can do' attitude.

Thanks to my work with Access Consciousness I also realize that creation, fun, and joy can also be part of business and it doesn't always mean that you have to work 20-hour days, especially if you are willing to follow the energy and receive a contribution from others. You don't have to do it alone. That is something I've learned over the last ten years. This makes a big difference in what can show up in your business and in your life.

Still, I am grateful for all the experiences I have had and would not trade any of them in for the world, even if it was not always pleasant. And believe me there have been many not-so-pleasant experiences along the way.

What makes a job or a work experience not-so-pleasant varies from person to person. It really depends on what is important to you.

What's important to me is fun, joy, kindness and respect, and yes, money too. Now each of those elements means something different to different people, but I know personally and professionally speaking a coherence and a flow between ease and personal satisfaction is fundamental.

When people ask me how to go about starting a business or how to turn a business into a profitable endeavor, I ask them in return: "What is fun for you? What is vital to you? What is it that without which you are merely going through the motions without the element of joy? What is it that you do that gets you so excited and involved that you forget to eat or sleep because you can't wait to get back to the playing field?"

When I decided to start my business, I did some real soul searching to find out what that was for me. I continually ask myself that question, week to week. I would love to say it is day to day, but sometimes, in the day to day, you have to execute tasks, get things done to put in place the elements that will create more ease and flow in the future. This is not always fun, but if you are clear that it will create more for you in the future, it is also a vital part of keeping your business current in an ever-changing world.

I had dedicated my life to helping others create more in their lives and businesses. I always chose jobs and projects because there was an underlying good intention that was congruent with attitudes and possibilities that I wanted to support and see more of in the world.

However, almost without exception, sooner or later, these business- es and jobs would lose sight of those good intentions and attitudes and possibilities and would become routine, without joy, without connectivity and with the sole purpose of making money or staying afloat. This is also important but when it becomes the sole objective then it limits the growth that is possible and eventually begins a cycle of death in a business, just as in life. I've seen it happen time and time again. When you keep your vision, present and allow that vision to contribute and guide you, then what you create has a con- tinual source of life and ease and the magic has a place to contribute to you and the carrying out your vision.

When I realized that most people and companies somewhere along the way lose their vision as the driving force, I realized that may- be it was time to start a business of my own, one that worked for me. As the overachiever that I am, I started several different busi- nesses (why just one?). All these businesses were based on the products that I had experience promoting and developing over the years: film, theater, events. I was very idealistic and thought I could change the world using these projects as a starting point. In short, it didn't work out the way I had hoped for one simple reason: I didn't realize that at the core of a business is also the product. If the prod- uct or project is not part of the vision, then the project has no light.

One day it dawned on me: if I were to give that kind of dedication to a project of my own, what would that look like? What would be the product? What did I have to develop and promote? I pondered on this for a while and even asked some friends and colleagues for input. It took me a while to hear what they all were saying. It seemed like just fluff and nothing concrete. Then I realized that what I was calling fluff and non-concrete, the project, that product which would be an added value to promote, what they were all talking about was ME.

They all knew me in personal and professional situations and the one thing that they all said was how valuable it was to them to have my input, my ideas, my approach to life as a resource for them in their relationships and in their businesses. I finally considered that maybe, just maybe, making ME and my approach to life was the product of my own business. How to share that with the world, the magic of me, that was the element I had been unwilling to see, the key to my success and the light on the road to the pursuit of happiness.

Starting a new business

Starting a new business that works for you is something that everyone approaches in a different way. Most people don't even consider the possibility that a business can be fun, that it can work for you, fit your desires and make you money all at the same time. In this reality you usually have to give up the idea of fun, give up the idea of making money or give up you. What if there was a different way of doing it?

A few years ago, after years of working to grow other people's businesses and also having a couple of mediocre successes with my own start-ups, I decided to begin seeking ways to make this reality work for me.

Somehow, I felt that it was egotistical, or exposing myself too much. The concept of failing or not having great success when you have a product or an event that has you as the focus was a little scary.

What if I don't succeed? Would that mean that I as a person am not a success? That I myself would be the failure more than the business itself being the failure, since I WAS the business.

This had me questioning all my beliefs about myself, what I had to offer and if I, as a product, was marketable, useful and translatable into a "product" that others would deem satisfying and worth spending time and money on.

What I knew is that I had a lot of different experiences. I didn't just have varied experiences, but I had experiences that were different from those of other people. This realization would be the key to my success, whether or not the business had success, I as a person would be successful once I realized that. Still, it took me a while to realize that.

The fact of having worked, lived, and loved in different countries, in different languages and in different positions made me extremely marketable.

Being able to present yourself and what you do to different a variety of people means you have a lot more to choose from. The problem was that by most accounts, the key to any successful business is finding your niche, your ideal customer, your specific field of expertise, and your target geographical area.

By my very nature I have made friends and contacts around the world and, as I said before, in different languages.

So, thinking about the rule number one in business (niche, target customer, and demographic) I knew that if I wanted to have success following those rules I would have to narrow my very nature down to one niche, one type of customer, and one geographical area.

This is where the problem came in. How the heck do you do that? What criteria do you use to eliminate the people, places and languages you know and love' How do you ascertain where your skills will be most appreciated? Some books and schools of thought even concede you the leeway to grow your business, expand you zone of influence into different areas, different niches and target different people but only after a while. They all seemed to agree that you have to start somewhere, follow the one niche, one field, one ideal customer, one language and one geographical are rule, at least at the beginning.

When I looked at this, it began to make me feel...smaller.

The one thing I had promised myself, after working with people whose vision dwindled after a while, is that I would not limit myself or reduce my personality for anyone. If I couldn't create a business that worked for me, I might as well find a job and make lots of money and enjoy my vacations like the rest of the world.

So, reducing my areas of interest to "one niche" or "one country" or "one language," for me was to do just that, limited myself and frankly I wasn't up for it.

I had been teaching classes and workshops based on the tools of Access Consciousness for over for almost ten years when I decided to start my business and, so I decided to use those very tools to create a business that worked for me.

What is fun for me?

What would work for me?

What energy, space, and consciousness could I be that would allow me to create a business and a life in this reality but that went beyond this reality?

These are the questions I asked and continue to ask daily about my life and my business. The response I get each time I ask this question talks about "being everything I am without excluding anything."

So, I started my journey to building my business without excluding anything.

I did classes in different countries, in different languages, and talked about a variety of topics: business, money, relationship, body, race, energy, family, and me.

I started traveling, contacting my friends and telling them what I was doing. I was doing so much that most of them couldn't "get their mind around" what exactly I did. That is what it means to create beyond this reality.

This reality is so busy categorizing and defining and pigeon-holing people and proposals and offerings that if you are beyond those categorizations or continue to add more meat to the fire, they somehow don't know what to do with you.

The temptation to give in to this need to define my work was present, but each time I tried, I wasn't able to "break it down" to one or two topics, one or two countries and one category of people.

I realize that people who want to start a business are looking to find the perfect fit, where do they and their talents fit. They often do this without having the full picture of what's out there. Most people do a little shopping and then settle for the most bright and shiny object or the one that "statistically speaking" or "what most people recommend."

Statistics are based on set of criteria. Recommendations are based on a set of criteria. By their very nature 'criteria' do not encompass everything you are or everything you know or everything you have to offer.

I choose to use questions as my criteria. I choose a topic, location or language based on the response I get from the questions I am asking at the time. Where I should go, what I should talk about and who shows up are the people who are looking for what I am offering at that time, even if they have no idea what that is.

Sometimes lots of people show up, sometimes no-one shows up. I am never dissuaded. As long as I am following what I know and being true to me, I am a success and my business is a success.

Working with other people

If you are a great connector, or if people think you have a great product, they offer to help you out and think they want to join your business.

Sometimes it works out, sometimes it doesn't. Since I love working with people, on teams and creating with interesting people, I am always up for adding people to my projects and collaborating with others.

Like I said, sometimes it works out, sometimes it doesn't. Especially when you really like someone, it is not always easy to remain impartial and part ways just because they have a different vision. This is where real honesty with yourself is required and also a trust in what you know and an honoring of you and the business and of the other person. Not projecting your vision on to them, not expecting them to do things your way or even to understand what your vision is. They either get it, and have something to contribute, or they try to take your business off in a direction that they think is best or worse yet, put the brakes on.

I am always reminded of the song The Gambler: "You've got to know when to hold them, know when to fold them, know when to walk away, and know when to run."

I don't worry about losing people. I am willing to receive contribution from a variety of people but, so many people have fixed points of view about what business is supposed to look like and what constitutes success.

When it is their business, then I just have to ask myself what I can contribute to them with my brand of magic.

When it is my business I have to ask if there is something they can contribute to me with their brand of magic.

What is your criteria for success?

I remember once I was scheduled to do a tour in North America. I had three different cities on the schedule and the same host for all those cities.

As we got closer to the date, the city in which my host lived was the event that was growing the fastest and had the most amount of people.

When I asked questions about it, my host suggested that I cancel the other two locations since they were not growing.

That didn't match the vision I had for the tour or my business. What I got was that my going to all three cities, whether or not people showed up, was more in line with what I wanted to share with the world.

I had no idea what it was going to look like but I chose to go to all three cities even if no-one was showing up.

The other two cities, that I had been advised to cancel, had much less attendance than the first city, my host's home town. In fact, there were only 6 people in one of the cities and by her economic and logical criteria it was not a successful event. But at that scarcely attended event one gal from another country showed up. A week after the class she called me and invited me to come do an event in her country.

Six months later, I went to Japan, her country, and held a very successful event, with the largest attendance record to date.

What appears to be a bad idea may simply be based on a different vision, a lack of vision or the criteria that someone else has made up which has nothing to do with you and what you know and where you want to go.

If you want to know what the best move for you is, what will work for you, what will create more in your life and in your business, you have to ask questions.

You have to be willing to go beyond the categories, criteria and logic and follow what you know to be true about you and about the world.

No one has the same thing to offer as you do.

No one presents the same possibilities as you do.

If you trust your intuition, your gut feeling, your sixth sense, you are knowing and are willing to ask questions which truly open up more possibilities from which to choose what will contribute more to you, your business and the world then you are already a success and when you are willing to trust you all the energies of the earth and the universe will delight in supporting you, your life and your business.

The Author

Kass Thomas

www.CreatingBusinessBeyondThisReality.com/kass-thomas

CHAPTER 4

Is Hard Work Giving You the Success You Deserve?

Georgia Watson

If you would like to create business beyond this reality, you will have to give up looking for it and start creating it. Everything that you put in place to look outside of you for the answer, or what could be, loops back to this reality. Would you be willing to choose different starting today?

What if you looked to you and what if you knew way more about business than you have ever acknowledged? This chapter is about finding what you're brilliant at and creating a business with ease and success; not from hard work, but with elegance. Does that sound like something you would like to have more of?

What is the difference between hard work and elegance in business?

Hard work

Hard work has built in limitations and judgments. How many of these ideas have you bought and sold over the years?

- You have to put in the hours
- Get your nose to the grind stone
- An honest day's work pays off
- If you work hard, you'll be rewarded
- You have to know the right people
- You have to get a college degree
- You're too young to do that
- You're too old to do that
- Get the right education and letters behind your name
- You *can't* be a woman in business or you *have* to be a woman in business
- Choose either family or a career
- With hard work and determination, you will succeed
- Get your piece of the pie
- Money doesn't grow on trees
- You have to spend money to make money
- It's not what you know but who you know

Do you notice how many absolutes and answers there are in this list? They also invite a constant state of judgment of you. If success in business required me to judge me constantly, I would not be having anywhere near the fun or success I have with business today. The sooner you see the lies in what reality says creates a successful business, the sooner you will be on your way to creating business beyond this reality.

Elegance

Now, what is elegance in business? Elegance is the least amount of effort used to create the greatest effect. This approach requires you to work smart, kindly (to you and often others), benevolently, and beyond this reality. Does this maximize profits? No. Maximize implies there is a maximum. What if your business, your profits, growth, and the fun you could have in business had no maximum, no limit?

Anywhere you bought the idea there is a maximum amount of money you or your business could have, would you give that up?

Business in this reality is supposed to be some nearly impossible to achieve combination of hard work, good luck, and knowing the right people, but what is businesses beyond this reality? Business beyond this reality is working with your strengths, with your aptitudes, and with what comes naturally to you. One problem is that many of the change agents, seekers of the world, people like you and me, believe that what comes most easily is the least valuable thing we have to offer. Striving and conquering challenges is far more celebrated than looking at the innate brilliance that each person has in unique areas. Elegant business is seeing what has great value in what you have, do, and be that others cannot have, do and be.

Are you willing to see that there is greatness in you that no one else could ever be, do, or have?

What if there is brilliance in even the things that you have judged yourself the most harshly for? What if every wrongness of you is a strongness of you? And would you be willing to ask and receive money for anything you have judged is wrong about you?

If you are looking at starting a new business or adding new income streams to your life, ask the universe, ask you, or ask your friends the following questions:

"What is something I'm good at, have ease with, and excel at that I've never fully acknowledged that has a value* to others?"

NEVER confuse the price you charge, what people pay for your product or service as *your* value. I have found in my business coach-

---

*The "value" aspect is about looking at if there is a market out there for what you are offering. Are there people somewhere around the globe that would likely pay for your product or service?

ing practice that those who have a hard time pricing their goods or services have confused their business, product, or service with their own worth. My close friend, Simone Milasas, is a brilliant business woman who teaches classes all over the world called *Joy of Business*. She introduced me to this idea. What if everything you were paid for was not a reflection of your worth, but a gratuity for you being you?

If you looked at pricing in your business that way would it make you more money? Would business be more fun and less significant? You know!

Make a brilliance list. Get these brilliances you have down in list form. You do not need to do anything with the list necessarily, but grow it, acknowledge the brilliance you are, and that allows for even greater to show up. This can surely include brilliances that you thought were awful and terrible about you. Are you brilliant at getting "hangry" (that is when you are so hungry that you get angry)? Write it down too!

How does this tie in with elegance? Elegance in business is the willingness to use anything and everything to your advantage. It's the willingness to see that you are not wrong. Elegance in business is the willingness to forge (not force) ahead and create a life and living that works for you, and in turn ask and receive the universe working for you and with you to create the reality beyond this reality that you know is possible.

And what about so-called savant capacities?

One thing to start looking at we often take for granted is what comes most easily to us. Sometimes these are called savant capacities. Do you have any that you have not acknowledged? I've lost track of how many times I've had conversations where I see someone has a natural ability and they can't imagine that others do not have it too. It is almost unfathomable that not everyone else, or most everyone else possesses the same talent. But if you change that little oversight and begin to celebrate what makes you uniquely you, and what you are innately superior at, that's the beginning of elegant, brilliant, and lucrative business.

If you would like to play with your brilliance list even more, take one thing that you are brilliant at and do a little brainstorming. What professions could possibly use this capacity? Note: This is not about defining what your next career move is. It is about seeing that you are a gift, that your natural capacities are a gift, and that your gifts can contribute to infinite income streams in your life.

For example, if one thing on your list is "Keeping people's secrets is easy for me". This lends itself to many professions.

> Therapist
>
> Life Coach
>
> Hair dresser
>
> Courier
>
> Escort
>
> Spy
>
> Undercover police officer
>
> Keeper/protector of secret recipes
>
> And I wonder what else?

Consider also that there are thousands of professions out there that you may never have heard of, like professional gift wrapper, LEGO builder, planetarium technician, and professional smeller, to name a few.

Whether these interest you or not, the important thing is to realize that there are possibilities for business, work, and income streams that are outside of what you've ever imagined. Would you be willing to ask for possibilities beyond what you have imagined starting to show up in your life?

What if each morning for the next week you started the day asking,

- Universe, will you show me something beyond what I ever imagined possible?

- What talents, abilities, and brilliance do I have that I have never acknowledged?

- And what can I add to my life today that would make me money right away and in the future?

Pragmatic Applications

What if working were fun? Would you do it more? I may work a lot, but I work with joy. When I have many tasks I need to get done, I choose whichever is the most fun at that moment. Usually what seems the easiest and most exciting to tackle first is where there is the energy of creation just waiting for me to engage with it.

There might be a point where I get down to 3-5 tasks I don't want to do, but that's when I ask a question. Is now the time? If the answer is no I look at it and ask, is it true I need to do this today or is there another possibly? Usually my to-do list will "ping" or talk to me when it is time to make progress on one or more of my projects. What if you had so many projects in the works that there was always something fun for you to work on, create with, or add to? What can you add to your life today that would make you money now and in the future?

And it is a strange, but wonderful law of the universe that money follows joy. Would you be willing to ask the universe to show you joy with your work?

There is a Difference Between Ease and Easy

Easy is where you avoid doing the things you've already decided are hard. Ease is where you can complete even the most difficult tasks with joy, elegance, and grace.

When things get hard in business or in any area of life ask,

What's possible here that I haven't considered?

What is one way around this? What's another way? Are there more ways around this than I thought?

I don't know about you, but no one ever told me that work could be easy, fun, lucrative and be an impetus to grow as a person and being. If you stopped looking for what was easy and began creating what would create ease for you, would that change the way your business showed up?

Making Business Decisions

One area that I have seen trip up my business coaching clients over and over is when it comes to making decisions. There is a lot of weight put on choosing the right choice. What does that create? The right choice is not always what will create more money, peace, possibilities, anything else you would like more of. Elegance in business is about choosing what works for you and your business, not necessarily what is right. Instead of looking for the right choice, try asking,

• If I do this or if I choose this, will it make me money?

• If I choose this, what will it create?

Play with how that choice feels in your world. Does the energy around it lighten up?

Is it a little scary/exciting/beyond what you "should" choose? Hopefully so! Begin to develop your awareness of energy as you make choices and very soon choosing for your business and your life will shift from a source of frustration to an exciting exploration of what could be.

No one knows more about you and your business than you do. Be willing to ask experts, read and inform yourself about your options, but never give up your point of view or what you know for what someone else knows. No matter how successful, famous, or right an expert thinks they are, they do not know all that you know. What works for them may not work for you. The same goes with what I have presented here. Take the pearls that might contribute to you having the life and business you desire to have and know that you are the expert and creator of your life and business.

The Author

Georgia Watson

www.CreatingBusinessBeyondThisReality.com/georgia-watson

CHAPTER 5

Confessions of a Serial Entrepreneur

Peggy Sue Honeyman-Scott

Yes, it's true, I can't stop creating. Nothing is more exciting to me than the beginning stages of bringing a new idea to life.

The businesses I have created include a Rock 'n' Roll clothing store in Dallas Texas (Dressed to Kill), a cookbook published in 1989 (Rock 'n' Roll Cuisine), a vegetarian catering company (Incredible Edibles), a line of yoga mat bags and underwear (Deities), aromatherapy body lotions and bath salts (Deities), sexy Vargas inspired zodiac tee shirts (Deities), a line of feel good art cards (Sliced Moon Productions), a vegan snack (Zenergy Powerball's — sold in sixty Wholefoods stores) and a cashmere poncho company (Lilac Chili).

When I was a child no one encouraged me to do or be anything. The only thing my dad said was "If you don't go to college you'll never amount to anything". Thanks for that big old fat conclusion that lingered into my adulthood, Dad. I did go to college for six months just to make sure I amounted to something. He never mentioned any length of time, he he.

People Magazine was first published in 1974 and I became an avid reader. The pages were full of life stories of celebrities and non-celebrities alike who started from nothing, overcame adversity and became successful. Every week I read cover to cover the stories that were so inspiring and it kept me fueled. If they can do it, I thought, why can't I?

I remember reading in one such story a sentence that stuck with me forever. *If you keep putting one foot in front of the other, eventually you'll get there.* Not exactly sage material but it was just the image I needed to keep me going at the hardest of times.

Have you ever let fear stop you from creating the business you've always dreamed of? What if there was a way to create business with ease, joy and fun? Would you be willing to choose it now?

Many a light bulb had gone off before I created my first business. I would share my ideas with everyone to see if they thought it was a good idea and before I knew it someone grabbed it and ran with it. I learned a valuable lesson. If it feels light it doesn't matter what people think, do it anyway!

Light and Heavy

Every one of my businesses had a light energy. What do I mean by that? Light means it's true for you and heavy means it's a lie. When I first learned this Access Consciousness tool I didn't get it. After six months of hopelessly trying to feel it in my body with no result, I finally asked some friends how they perceived light and heavy. One person explained to me that to them they saw YES for light and NO for heavy in neon flashing lights. For another it was heavy if they felt a pain in their left knee. (my knees are fine) For me it is a combination of words, sensations, and most often a knowing.

What if you practiced asking what is light and heavy for everything you do? Wouldn't it be fun to be able to perceive the energy?

Gary Douglas the founder of Access Consciousness™ has numerous businesses that he checks in with each day to see what needs attention. Surprisingly not all of them do. Each day is different and each business requires different things at different times, so don't forget to ask them questions.

Following the Energy

What if this became the normal way to operate a business? What if you threw out your lists and asked questions and followed the energy instead? What do I mean by this? Instead of making a 'to do' list of things you think you *have* to do, when something comes to mind, do it. It might mean going for a walk in the middle of the day when you think you 'should' be working. Or calling a friend you haven't thought of for ages? What if on that walk you bumped into someone who wanted to contribute to your business in some way? What if an idea came to you while speaking to your friend? This practice helps connect you to your inner knowing. How much fun can you have following the energy?

Conclusion versus Question

I love looking in the dictionary for the meanings of words, they can be deceivingly different especially when you look at the root.

The definition of CONCLUSION is: A judgement or decision reached by reasoning. Every time you come to a conclusion you are slamming the door to possibilities. Does that feel light or heavy? What will it take for you to catch yourself every time you come to a conclusion and change it into a question?

After a lifetime of bad programming I've got to be on my toes to catch myself numerous times a day! The more you practice the more aware you will become of how much or little you and others are functioning from conclusion.

The definition of QUEST is an act or instance of seeking and TION indicates an action, process, or creation. So, are you seeking action by asking a quest-tion? I was so excited when I saw this, not only was it incredibly light, there is so much more going on than waiting for an answer. I imagine the question floating through the air changing ions and molecules into the future! What would it take to live in the question that keeps endless possibilities flowing? Sometimes the awareness is front and center and other times it will show up in a week or a month or a year. Notice I used the word awareness instead of answer. If you stay open to the possibilities magic will show up in ways you could never imagine and couldn't have possibly figured out. Whatever you do stay curious and don't stop asking!

What would it take for it to be easy for you?

Business Plans

There is no right way to start a business and I would guess that there are just as many ways as there are people. Here are the general rules for creating business in the usual reality.

Step 1: Write a Business Plan

Step 2: Get Business Assistance and Training

Step 3: Choose a Business Location

Step 4: Finance Your Business

Step 5: Determine the Legal Structure of Your Business

Step 6: Register a Business Name ("Doing Business As")

Step 7: Register for State and Local Taxes

Step 8: Obtain Business Licenses and Permits

Step 9: Understand Employer Responsibilities

Step 10: Find Local Assistance

Now does that list feel light or heavy? For me, just reading this list makes me tense up! What if you could get everything you need without following the rules of that reality? Someone somewhere came up with this list so what if you made your own list?

Business plans were created for banks and investors and the problem with business plans is that they are constantly changing. My business partner and I created one for our food business and with every new bit of information we changed it (which was every day).

What if you could create the perfect business plan the bank needed to see so that you could get the loan you require? While you are creating a plan ask questions like: What does the bank want to see that will make them want to give me a loan?

I'll give you some examples of how I created my businesses with and without the Access Consciousness tools, none of which is right or wrong it's just the way I went about it. All of them were created from joy as I love being in space of creative energy.

The Beginning

My first business was in 1982. I'd been traveling back and forth from London to Texas. Every time I was stateside and went out in public people would complement me on my clothing and ask where they could buy them. BHAM! An idea was born! I decided to open a shop importing Rock 'n' Roll clothing from London. I had no idea what it would entail but the energy of it was so light and FUN, I just had to do it! I brainstormed with some friends and came up with the name "Dressed to Kill". BHAM! It was such an electric energy.

The internet and computers were not around at that time, so I asked other business owners I knew how they started and what I heard over and over again was, you MUST create a business plan! I had no idea what a business plan was. What I did have was a small budget and an 'I'm gonna do it' attitude. But there were other's I talked with and asked how they began and they said, 'I just had this idea and did it.' Excuse me? Aren't there some steps in the middle there? It was like they had a secret and did not want to share it.

Next was finding the location. I made a conclusion right away in that I wanted to be in a city that I didn't know many people. (My husband had passed away eight months previously and I wanted to start afresh). I did <u>not</u> ask the business where it would like to live. What might it have created had I been in a city where everyone knew me? What might it have created had I not jumped to a conclusion?

Saying that, magic still occurred. I was driving to meet a real estate agent to view properties, and out of the corner of my eye I caught a 'FOR RENT' sign in the window of a vacant shop that was *not* in the area I was told would be 'right'. BHAM! I did not know Dallas at all and yet knew this was where my shop would be. I went through the motions of seeing all of the other properties, but I ended up with the first one I 'accidentally' found.

Enlisting a friend to help me install carpet, build a wall and a desk, I painted the walls myself, bought a used clothing rack and slowly sold and restocked until the eight hundred square foot shop was filled with clothing and shoes. It was ticking along quite successfully for three years until suddenly without warning the landlord sold the building without my knowledge. The new owners tripled my rent. Instead of asking questions and possibly staying or changing locations I came to the conclusion that it was too expensive, and it was a sign for me to move on.

Had I known the Access Consciousness tools I would have asked more generative questions...

> Business, do you want to keep selling clothes?
>
> Business, where would you like to move?
>
> If I move the store what will my life be like in 5 years?
>
> If I close the store what will my life be like in 5 years?

It was 1986 when I closed the store and moved back to the UK. I had great connections with jewelry companies for my Dallas store, so I had the idea to rent a small booth to sell at an antique market in London. My friend Robin decided at the last minute to accompany me to meet the landlord. We showed up at the arranged time and sat on the steps for thirty minutes as we waited for him (he never showed up). She shared an idea with me about compiling recipes from musicians for a cookbook. It has so much energy it was like a lightning bolt struck me in the head! I said, "This is IT, we are doing this, let's go!"

We never looked back. We asked a flurry of questions and 'Rock 'n' Roll Cuisine' was born. Without computers at that time we managed to create a book with 98 pages of fun filled original recipes accompanied with drawings and snapshots of the likes of Rod Stewart, Mick Jagger, Fleetwood Mac and many more.

We used the phone book to gather manager's numbers, called friends of friends and went out to bars and concerts where we talked to everyone about it. It was easy for us because they were our circle of friends. Robin's husband was in a band and so had been mine so that helped. We had a logo designed and printed on our typed-out letters (yes, the old-fashioned way one at a time) mailing each in the Royal Mail.

It was on all accounts a huge success. Scheduled to be a TV show, we had spin offs for greeting cards and everything else, but it fizzled out after the recession hit the UK. Once again, we stopped asking questions and came to the conclusion that the recession would affect us negatively!

I continued coming to conclusions with several of my other businesses until I had my first Access Consciousness™ class. Here it was suggested that I write my ideas on a piece of paper and ask each one of them, "When would you like to be created?" I was excited about the idea of the cashmere business but when I asked the question I got that it wanted to be created in eight months. Did I hear EIGHT MONTHS? Nooooo! I was not happy with the answer, I wanted to get moving on it straight away, but it was loud and clear, so I decided to trust it. I continued with the other projects I'd been working on and at the eight month mark the cashmere sort of slapped me in the face – after I'd long forgotten it.

This time I never stopped asking conscious questions. In doing so, my cashmere company, Lilac Chili evolved in ways I never expected and it keeps surprising me. At times in the designing of the pieces I would come to a roadblock. I would speak to the cashmere and say, 'Ok, I'm going to have a cup of tea and when I get back, would you please let me know what you want to be?' Material was put together in a way I could never have figured out, and it was pure magic.

The three-year mark is the usual time I get bored in my businesses and give up but this time I chose to ask more questions. "Business, do you want to keep creating? What else can we do that I have not thought of yet?" I was surprised again that it wanted to keep going, and I didn't have to close it to move onto other things. I've slowly built the company and to this day it is still a joy to me.

Generative Questions

Generative questions are gateways to inquiry. Focus questions shape learning and explorative questions direct learning. Each type of question has a particular value, role and function in learning. When they are used in combination, they become powerful and empowering beyond words. Here are examples of some starter questions.

> Is this idea light or heavy?
>
> Will you make me money?
>
> Will this be fun for me?
>
> When do you want to be created?
>
> What do you want to be?
>
> If I choose this will it expand my life and my business?
>
> Who do I need to speak to?
>
> What do I need to do?
>
> Who can help me with marketing?
>
> What role is easy for me?
>
> What else is possible here that I have not thought of yet?
>
> What will it take to expand into other areas?
>
> Who can I find to fill the other roles? What will my life be like in five years if I create this?

What will my life be like in five years if I don't create this?

What if there was no such thing as failing?

What if you took that one step (like asking a question) towards creating your business today?

What else is possible? ®

The Author

Peggy Sue Honeyman-Scott ©
www.CreatingBusinessBeyondThisReality.com/
peggy-sue-honeyman-scott

CHAPTER 6

What to Do when Investing in your Business Doesn't Pay Off

JENNIFER CRAMER LEWIS

Recently I had a client message me in tears, she said "Hello lovely Jennifer, millionaire Goddess! Since our course, things shifted, and I increased my income. And then I launched my new website, did amazing work on my business and really followed my passions in my work. However, along the way, I am further in debt and am riddled with guilt and failure as Hubby is working away to make ends meet. I almost feel like, I will never attract or receive money because it has never showed up for me. What am I missing? What am I subconsciously deep-down blocking or not honoring? Many thanks."

This client is open and willing to make many changes in her life and was truly puzzled when the choices that she made for her business did not pay off the way that she thought that they would or should.

I am an Access Consciousness Certified Facilitator®, I teach people to ask questions to get an awareness of what is true for them in their business, their body, their families and in their whole life.

What happens when you act on your own awareness in business?

Acting on your own awareness in business gives you a stronger platform on which to stand. In today's marketplace there are dozens of messages every hour sent to us about how "this thing" is the thing that is going to launch your business to the next level, if you just this next super-duper sales funnel, this exact way of approaching your clients, this office, this new modality... the list is endless. When you learn to ask questions to "this thing" you are considering investing in for your business, the awareness that you sense can not only save you money... it could actually make you some too! How does that sound?

TIP ONE   Are you willing to know that investing in your business is investing in your future?

One of the laws of attraction is that we get more of what we focus on. If you focus on paying your bills and that the money coming in is somehow lacking, then what do you get? More bills and money that is less than the bills.

What can you do with that? There is a formula that states if you take 10% of your income and put it into a savings account just for you, and **never spend it**, that it will change your financial income. What that does is *pays you first*. Then your money reality gets accustomed to being paid first, before the bills. Another thing that this formula does, is when your savings accumulate to a substantial amount for you, you start getting accustomed to *having money* and getting out of lack. How does that sound?

Personally, it took me a long while after being aware of this formula to implement it. Once I did implement it, my financial reality changed dramatically for the better. In fact, only 6 short years ago, I was $50,000 in debt not including the mortgage I had on my townhouse that was not worth the amount on the mortgage!

Today, I pay off my credit cards each month and live in a beautiful home we call "The Country Mansion" and it doesn't have a mortgage. I am grateful beyond measure for what choices I have made to change my financial situation for the better. I honour and acknowledge that this was not luck or karma, it was the sum total of the willingness to choose and implement choice in my life. I asked for change and received it when it came. I still do, every day.

So, investing in you, is investing in your business.

TIP TWO   Make a list of all the investments that you have made in you and your business over the last 12 months. Let's ask that list some questions... without right or wrong.

1. Does this investment make me feel bubbly and happy or something else?

When you have a look at the investment does it make you feel something to have it or have used it or taken part in it? Does it make you feel bubbly or light or happy when you think about what you got out of having this investment in your business or life? Say you took a course or a series of courses, how do they make you feel when you re-listen to them? If you feel something other than bubbly or happy, what is that feeling? Check into that, if it makes you feel guilty or heavy or that you wasted your money, then ask another question. *Is this heavy feeling even mine?* Yes or No? If it isn't yours or a portion of it isn't yours then you can send the heaviness back to the person who sent it to you. You simply say, "Return this to Sender" and be aware that the feeling wasn't yours. You were picking it up on your internal WIFI. Access Consciousness invites us to consider that up to 98% of what we are picking up does not originate with us, so perhaps the thought that your business investment didn't show up the way you planned is one of those "not mine" places?

2. What future did I create with this investment?

Pause and be aware of the future that you created by making the investment in the first place. What other possibilities or opportunities showed up by way of making this investment? Did you meet someone? Did you have another product idea or create something else in your business? Did you get out of your comfort zone and created more opportunities to get out of your comfort zone that you were able to choose? ***Did you jump up a few levels in your willingness to ask for more to show up in your life and business?*** If all of this or some of it feels true, perhaps what you created in your business isn't showing up like you expected it to. Often, we have preconceived notions of what investing in our business looks like and also what the ideal end result will be. This closes off what you really can receive because unless it looks exactly like what you have already predetermined it to look like, then you don't see what future you did create. What would it be like to tap into what you really did create and ask that to show up more dynamically. So, ask this question daily:

3. Who was this investment for, me or someone else or something else?

Sometimes when we make an investment in our business we do it for ourselves and sometimes we do it for others and sometimes we do it for something else entirely. Asking this question will bring about an awareness of who the investment really was for. For example, when I got the awareness that living in Vancouver no longer worked for me, it wasn't a giant blow up. It was a quiet tap on the shoulder that we could choose to move and that it might be an ideal time to do so. When I asked Tom if he would consider moving, he said yes, and it was a super easy choice for both of us. All our friends thought we were crazy for moving so far away but the choice was so easy to make that it defied everyone's expectations of us. We sold our home in a downward market for top dollar in one day. The investment in our new country home seemed to be for me because I was the one with the idea to move out of the city, I was the one who wanted land and a garden. Now that we are here, I can see that the awareness to move included Tom and our entire families, also our friends, my clients, Tom's clients, our new community that we are becoming a part of, everyone is benefiting from this investment. Another perspective, did you make the investment as proof of something? Did you do it for the credentials that it would give you or perceived expertise? I see so many coaches, including myself in the past, that were chasing gold stars as a way of proving to themselves or perspective clients or even their families that they are a "good coach". ***What would it be like if you didn't have to prove anything anymore, especially with your bank account?*** Making an investment for something else looks like this. What if all the people in your industry have these certain things that they do, and you are caught in a paradigm where you simply "have to have this"? Asking a question like "Who was this investment for?" will give you the awareness. Then you can ask more questions.

4. *What else is possible with this investment now?*

Perhaps when you made the investment you were not quite ready to take advantage of it. What investments in your business are you now ready to make full use of? How many times have we bought things for our business and then didn't know how to use them at their full potential and kind of forgot about them? What if you could use them now? Also, what things did you learn or choose to make an investment in and are now ready to take full possession of and use?

Is there another way to use the thing that you invested in? Can you loan it out? Who else would like to be able to use it? For example, the country mansion has the capacity to be used as a BnB, a retreat centre for myself or Tom or to be used by other coaches or businesses. Asking the question opens up possibilities that you may not have immediately considered. I asked this question to one of my clients who had a great healing space in her home and she chose to have another business come into her space to do aesthetics sessions. What other profitable possibilities are available with this investment now?

TIP 3   Be willing to let it all go.

What if it really was a not so bright moment when you made the investment in your business? What if it never did pay off in a multitude of thousand-dollar deposits to your bank account? If you are willing to let it go and make it not mean anything about you or the business "being bad" for not showing up the way you want it to, then the possibilities really are limitless for something cooler and more profitable to show up for you. Like I said above, when we judge the results or ourselves, what we get is more of what we judge. Can you really let it all go? Here are some questions to ask so that you can see if you are in your head or using your whole awareness.

Question: Truth, what percentage of this thing is in my head? What percentage of it is in my body?

Access Consciousness has over 60 body processes that can be done in client sessions to release energetic build up in bodies. When you are stressed about something in your life or business it takes its toll on your body. Headaches, pains in the neck, stresses on the joints, organs, nervous system are some of the ways that work stress gets stuck in your body. Regular energetic body work will keep your body free of the stress that is building up and can't get out without assistance. While Access Consciousness is not the only energy alignment that you can choose, it has been for me, the only one that created long lasting relief from anxiety and depression. There are Access Consciousness facilitators and practitioners worldwide in 174 countries and counting.

Question: Truth, does letting go of these expectations expand my life or diminish it?

When you think of your whole life, if you let go of the expectations that your business was going to show up exactly how and when you demand it to, what would it create? Do you get a sense of it getting larger or smaller when you tap into it? Remember these questions are about creating or accessing an awareness, not an answer. This one is more energetic. Does your life and living get bigger or smaller? Does it work for you when people have expectations of you or does it feel like you have to measure up? What about having expectations of your business? Does it feel like your business has to measure up too? What if you let it all go? All of the expectations? Remember expectations are not targets or goals for your business.

Question: Truth, where could I go or what could I do today to create a different business reality right away?

Are you willing to let yourself have a couch day? Sometimes when I have a contracted feeling, I ask this question to myself and the awareness is that the couch is my ideal destination for the day. Not pushing through it or shoving my marketing onto the internet or cold calling clients, just giving myself a day off. Are you willing to give yourself an entire day off? What would that create for you?

Did you ever notice that some days it takes 3 hours to get something that ordinarily would take 20 minutes to complete? These are the couch days! I like to wait until the days where I can "genie blink" my creations into my business and life. The days where it takes 20 minutes to create something that ordinarily it would take 3 weeks. Ask this question "Is now the time to write this book? Call these people? Do these tasks?" If no, then you can ask the Universe to ping or alert you when the time is. Not making it important but allowing a larger awareness of where your energy is best utilized and also the energy of the thing that is ready to be created.

Sometimes when I ask this question, the awareness that arrives for me is that getting out of the house will create the most for my business. Do you work for you and the only way you are meeting people is online or over the telephone? Does that work for your body? How much does your body love getting out and experiencing the best that your neighbourhood has to offer, that another City or even Country has to offer. I often find that I am my most creative for content creation when I am on a vacation. Who can you meet on these outside days? Ask a question like "Who can I meet today to bring more profit right away? or What 5 people can I meet today to have more fun in my business right away?" The willingness to act on the awareness is where the magic happens.

TIP 4   Never Give Up, Never Quit, Keep on Going Going Going.

Yes, I am aware that the last tip seems contrary to this one. How fun is that? What invitation never give up, never quit and keep on going going going presents is this: What do you know about your capacities on this planet? What do you know about other people and what they need? If you don't do it, will it be done, or will people miss out on the opportunity that you being you present to them?

Years ago I knew that there was something for me as a facilitator and a speaker asking people to choose more for themselves in their lives. I hired a coach to work with me and help me develop my speaking, part of the exercise was to stand on a big stage and receive the audience, which at that time was one of the larger audiences I had spoken for. Then it was to double that size in my perception, then triple and quadruple. The coach then asked us to come back and share what it was that we got by completing the exercise. What I received was that if I gave up my facilitation business and went back to the corporate world to have a job, it would make me an asshole. I know that sounds harsh and that was the exact awareness that I got. If I gave up or chickened out or took the easy path that it would be a disservice to the people who would only receive if I was the person presenting. I would be the one voice to get through to them and assist them in creating the reality that they had been asking for, even dying to create.

What if that is true for you? What if you being you, presenting what it is that is easy for you to present and create, is able to change the world for those people who are looking for you? Would you quit then? Knowing you are the only key for them?

TIP 5 Competition is crap.

I do a lot of networking for my business with networking groups like the Chamber of Commerce or business to business referral groups. Often, I will meet another coach, facilitator, author or speaker and they will say something like "Oh I am a coach, we are competing for the same clients" and I now say "Oh, are we?" and smile. Personally, I don't subscribe to the competition philosophy. Let's do the math on competition... I would do this with a client who was accidentally buying into competition. Of all the 7 billion people on the planet, who are looking for services like yours right now? Let's forget about geography, I have a global coaching and speaking business and so can you, it's just about setting up some simple systems.

Is it more or less than half of those people? Now, of that amount, who are looking for services like yours, how many of them can actually choose and pay for them? So let's say that's an eighth of that amount. So, of that eighth, how many of them are left? Is that enough clients for you?

In closing, I would love to leave you with this. What if are the only person on this planet, in this universe that has your unique perspective, your set of life experiences and your talents and capacities? Are you treating your business like a billion-dollar business filled with billion-dollar clients? If not, then perhaps there may be a few things to talk about?

The Author

Jennifer Cramer Lewis

www.CreatingBusinessBeyondThisReality.com/

jennifer-cramer-lewis

CHAPTER 7

It Is *You* Who Gets to Change the World

MELANIE MEADE

You are unique, you are brilliant beyond belief, you are pure magic! No one sees what you see, no one knows what you know and YOU create in ways people could never fathom.

We all have those moments. Moments of doubt, moments of despair, moments of inadequacy. Even when we are flying high and everything is going swimmingly we get those moments that are the outer reaches of our comfort zone. This is where it is being asked of us to step up, show up, be that brilliance we naturally be, to be a leader in our lives and move forward and be our difference and be the change the world is asking for!

Sometimes we end up making interesting choices. We sometimes choose to go backwards or stay stuck on distracting ourselves from our natural brilliance. We worry about will it work, what will people think, is there a market for this, will it make money, will it be successful?

Yet when you look a lot of the inventions we might not be able to live without now, as they create so much more in our lives, it took someone with enough craziness to take a chance on what they knew and pursue their desire to create something that would change people's lives! The lightbulb, central heating, plumbing – even the wheel! Yes at one stage these were revolutionary!

How many ways can we change the world? Sometimes it is looking at creating something greater when something isn't working. Sometimes its increasing pleasure or quality of life and the list could go on and on. There is no one way to change the world. Yet I insist on not fixing problems but maybe ask what else is possible when things are not working. Rather than fixing what is broken I often wonder are there other possibilities rather than getting stuck in what is wrong.

A problem is just when we are fixed on a set menu of outcomes. We are actually trying to control what will create more in the world rather than trusting our sheer brilliance and awareness and trusting that we know the choices we make will actually create more in the world.

It does not mean we sit back and allow things to fall apart but that moment you realize things are not working you ask what can you be and do to change it. Be it a personal situation or something out there in the world, it is about not getting caught up in what is and look at what's possible.

I was never sure of what I had to give. I came into the world all shiny and sparkly seeing the beauty and possibility until I didn't. I ended up feeling like a minority, not everyone saw the world the way I did. So it had to be me that didn't have it right so I tried everyone else way. That didn't work. I felt worthless and of no value. I grew up never belonging. I felt so alien and weird about everything. I did this reality particularly badly. I couldn't seem to get anything right.

What I learnt over the years is no matter how hard you try not to be you, you will never quite succeed! I would have never considered myself a high achiever. I had very low confidence, high anxiety and found everything overwhelming. Yet I know people who have achieved great things by this realties standards that I had never achieved and judged myself as less than until I noticed they were filled with self-judgement too. They still yearned for who they truly were. So we were all in the same boat in a funny kind of way.

Even when you can't see how brilliant you are others can see the gift of you. For me it was met with resistance and reaction by a lot and adored by a few. I did grow up with a lot of ridicule and reaction – turns out I was terrible at hiding who I truly was. I was the only person that pretty much couldn't see it.

People seeing my brilliance or who I truly was did not guarantee warm hugs and big welcomes. Some people are so resistant to being themselves and losing the judgement of what it means to be successful and happy and be the magic they truly be they will try and make you wrong, dumb you down and discredit you.

Here is the key piece of information – when you are truly being you and your brilliance without judgement or conclusion of what that looks like and what results it creates – it can only create more. You cannot do any harm to anyone or anything when you are truly being you. It's when we try not to is when we hurt ourselves and others.

When we decide we are doing better or worse it creates less. When we make people greater or less than us it creates less. You are not allowing you to be your greatness or them to be theirs. It stops everyone contributing to everything including the planet. It is filled with judgement and control until we get the greatest gift we are to ourselves, to others and the planet is being ourselves. Sounds quite simplistic but this is what I found to create the most change in my life.

I had no idea how to create the change I knew possible. I just knew there was something. The "how to" escaped me. I saw the way other people created and that didn't work for me, it was too linear, too regimented and had a list of requirements and results to ensure success. Ultimately the end result was popularity and I was terrible at that. I found people had to change who they were and only offer what was already out there that people could receive.

I felt isolated, yet at this stage of my life going on the adventure of being me felt a lot lighter to pursue. I had no idea what was going to show up and it was definitely the unpopular choice. I was the freak. But only because it could not be figured out how I created. It mystified people. They were almost afraid to ask at times. I challenged their reality. But I was okay with that I knew I wasn't going to stop.

It can sound all saintly wanting to create a change in the world. Does that mean you have to be like Mother Theresa?

My observation was that people craved a validation others disingenuously provided for them. People that didn't feel great about themselves and sought it – they needed help and fixing because they felt less than and people that wanted to feel great about themselves and feel valuable gave that validation sought – they helped, healed and inspired and none of it was real. It was a game of greater than and less than. All of this was provided because they did not believe that they were naturally brilliant no matter what. It was disempowering and it angered me. It was controlling and that angered me too. But all in all the giver and the taker saw themselves as less than. That angered me too. There had to be another way.

When I did not buy that way of creating I was pushed aside. It was okay. I was used to being the outsider and the underdog. I was no longer playing small. I was willing to be the outsider and the underdog if that's what being me and exploring what it is that I would like to create as my life and in the world looked like. Remember – you can do no harm when you choose from consciousness. "Consciousness includes everything and judges nothing" – wonderful words from Gary Douglas.

I had trouble with judgement for a while. I thought I was super judgmental. I beat myself up so bad for it. Turns out it was awareness. I am highly sensitive (I would be very certain you are too) and

I was just aware of how everyone else was feeling, how worthless they felt and the judgements they had that they could not create what they knew was possible. So once I acknowledged that people being mean or nasty meant nothing to me I did not need to go fight it or deal with it. I would just out create it. I was going to create my life. It was not going to stop me anymore and I sure as hell was not waiting for people to come with me on what I knew was true for me. At the same time none of it was relevant. Choosing forward was the key and not having any fixed destination. It was the adventure of living. It allowed for wonderful surprises to come my way and whatever didn't work would melt away. I no longer doubted me.

There was a moment in life I was grateful for that occurred just before I took that leap into the adventure of being me without apology! I had the most beautiful, gentle almost regal Nana. Her sparkly eyes, her radiant smile, her warm hugs and unconditional love would assure me everything was going to be okay. She would always tell you how much she loved you. Every single one of her grandchildren and great grandchildren were seen as absolute gifts to her. She adored each of us for exactly who we were, and there were quite a few of us! A woman so full of love. I had not seen much of that in my life. All she wanted was the best for every one of us and she wished it upon us constantly. The beauty of this was it was absent of judgement and condescension. It was the most beautiful way of being. I adored that about her. She was so graceful no matter what.

I would call to see her. Always greeted by a hug, she would look at you, take you in and smile. She saw everyone for who they truly were. She would very occasionally, as we had a cup of tea, turn and smile at me and ask very gently "when are you going to share your gift with the world?" and I would, without over thinking it, would reply "soon Nan" and she would smile, nod her head and continue to drink her tea.

I never over thought it, I never saw it as energetic or academic I just on some level knew what she was asking me. I knew she saw me for exactly who I was and I was grateful for that. She never sought to protect me or push me forward she just acknowledged me very simply and graciously.

Her birthday was the day after mine. An easy one to remember but also felt special to me growing up. On her 90th birthday she spent it in respite. Not because she was sick, it was like a break away for her, have some company and social interaction. The nurses fussed over her that day, she was made feel special by them but also by all of her family. A lot of us called in during various times of the day. I called with my son. She adored him, the eldest of the great grandchildren she called him the King. I found that funny because we called her the Queen. She sat in her chair by the bed with at least two birthday cakes, flowers and surrounded by cards! She chatted and smiled and allowed me assist her with things she would not have requested before. She allowed me care for her, just little things. But it was different. She exuded her usual grace and laughed at all the fuss and cried for her husband and children that were no longer here with her. She missed them dearly.

Time came for us to leave. I hugged and kissed her goodbye. As I went to push the door to leave the room this incredible tug came over me to turn back to look at her, before I did I swelled up inside and just knew. I turned back, she sat up straight like a Queen with her head high and shoulders back, her hands gently clasped together. She had a graceful regality about her. We looked each other in the eye and she nodded her head and I gave a smile of acknowledgment. I wanted to burst into tears. I wanted to run back and squeeze her so tight but it was time to go. Not only to go home but go and share that gift with the world. It was time, she knew and I did too.

I was filled with gratitude for her and sadness that we both knew this was the last time we were to physically meet. There was no indication that in 6 weeks or so she would become very briefly unwell and die within 48 hours. Her body literally just started to shut down.

We just both knew there and then that this was it and I was under no circumstances to see her again. I knew she allowed me to care for her that day to make the choice to not see her again somewhat easier and family went into to hospital when she fell ill to say good-bye to her.

Gracious in life she was gracious in death. A truly beautiful gift of a woman, inside and out.

Around this time I had made some choices that were going to change my life. They might have seemed like nothing at the time but now at this place in my life I knew I had started to make real choices to start my adventure on coming out of hiding not only from the world but from myself and unearth and unmask what it is I always knew was possible.

It had no definition for a very long time, I just kept choosing no matter how illogical it all seemed. The universe provided, whenever I required the money for something it would show up. I would meet people and get the information I required to take the next step.

One of the biggest learning curves for me was that everything you think you are not you are. If you think you can't do it might actually be that you do it different. So different people can't see or understand it as it is something they have never seen before.

That is what being an entrepreneur is all about! It is about being a leader, not to have followers but to go forward with what you know is true for you. The word entrepreneur is associated with the word "risk" like you have something to lose, that it is a perilous game. What if it was losing the limitations, trusting what you know and embracing your brilliance and uniqueness?

Go forward and create your reality as when you choose to do that you will naturally create change in the world. People are asking for it, they are asking for you. It is opening the door to possibilities they have never considered. The possibility of being themselves and they too can lead the world to greater possibilities. There is room for us all. Not one of us are the same. Competition need not exist.

You being you creates change. My Nana lived a simple life yet created waves in mine. She did not need to be loud and proud about it, or make money from it or tell people what to do. With her absence of judgement and inviting us to be all of who we were in the most gentle and unspoken fashion created so much change for me. Her capacity of unconditional love was amazing. It was something I had never seen before.

I thought I was not a lot of things. I struggled with convention, not that I was a rebel I just found it hard to get by like everyone else. I was shy and retiring, this world was loud and abrasive and filled with hatred, judgement and inadequacy. I was ridiculed when I couldn't do it like everyone else, my brain learned things differently. I was good at certain things and not great at others. I always judged myself more for what I felt I could not do.

Yet there are super powers in everything you think is wrong about you. I can be invisible in people's business which is an asset, I do not seek public validation in the creation of others business I desire for them to thrive and their brilliance get out into the world. I am now also exercising being out front, blowing my trumpet, which can be a bit bizarre at times but we all have something to gift to the world in many shapes and forms and it starts with acknowledgment that you are brilliant – plain and simple.

I had literacy difficulties, I was laughed at for how I read. I am now a number 1 bestselling author and content creator. I just do it different, I read different and you might or might not notice but the way I go about writing is my way and not the way I was taught. Once I allowed that it flowed and the difficulty diminished.

My gift is my unique way of seeing the world that can be transferred into anything that is fun for me to play with. To some I appear cold or aloof yet my gift is clarity. I can appear nervous when I talk fast it's actually speed, I don't have a lot of time for nonsense.

When I stopped buying other people's projections and judgements, I saw the gift in everything I thought was wrong.

So if there is nothing wrong with you, what is truly possible for you?

What if we all gave up on how things should be and trusted what we know?

If being an entrepreneur is risky, what if it was being willing to risk losing limitations and truly exploring a phenomenal life!

Are you ready to take the leap into something far greater than you could have ever imagined?

Being YOU sounds truly simplistic yet it is the most potent and game changing contribution to the world! My Nana showed me with no judgement or expectation you could change the world. She also showed me that words cannot always describe the beauty of what is possible for us here to live and be right now. You can't describe it – YOU BE IT!

The Author

Melanie Meade

www.CreatingBusinessBeyondThisReality.com/melanie-meade

CHAPTER 8

What They Won't Teach You in Business School

REBECCA HULSE

The debate on, if formal education for business is good for you or not, goes around in circles every day. "You need to know the components of a successful business structure" is met with example after example of successful business creators without a degree.

The truth is if you truly desire to do something, you can do it! Yes, it can help to educate yourself about what you desire to create (and you picked up this book so great job!) but a formal education can hinder as much as it can help you.

In the following exploration into what I have found most useful in creating multiple successful international businesses around the world is documented as best as I can in the following chapters. The tools and systems I use have come from a background in marketing, copious amounts of creativity and the incredible Access Consciousness tools.

Financial awareness

How many times have you run away from looking at money and your financial situation? Most people would rather tell a complete stranger a sexual experience than share how much they make!

When you receive a bank or credit card statement do you look at it and get more awareness about what you created last month financially or do you say you will look at this later.

In order to create a successful profitable business you need to be able to create your own financial awareness. Your business has its own financial reality – what is it like? Is it expanding with a generative energy with clear insight to what it's currently making and spending? Or is it in a jumble and you kind of know what's going on but haven't spent the energy to actually nourish and look at it?

For Joy of Business I have an amazing financial assistant, Laura who I call my "Money Buddy". We are in a constant conversation with the financial reality of Joy of Business and asking, "What else is possible?®".

Incessantly asking and looking for new possibilities to show up, bringing Joy of Business into higher levels of profit and being aware of all the different moving pieces of this business allows us to be clear when making choices. We know what will and won't work financially, we don't always base out choices on this because we are also simultaneously looking at what will expand Joy of Business as a whole. We never ignore the financial reality though.

And funnily enough your own person financial reality has to expand too It's a wonderful way to trick yourself into being willing to create and receive more money – how terrible!

Creative Accounting

Can you truly say you love accounting? Looking at a spreadsheet, seeing everything balance correctly? Or did I lose you at the start of this section?

If you're not enthused by the subject you are talking to the wrong accountant! If I could set you any home-play from this chapter it would be to challenge you to find an accountant you truly love. You can set up a consultation with any accountant before taking them on, ask them questions, see if there's an energy of creativity, smarts and dare I say it JOY in the conversation. Are they condescending or willing to explain things to you and work together. These are some of the elements to look for.

I happen to have inherited an amazing one through my family. Growing up hearing stories of my dad starting a new company for every idea he had, almost 5 years later now we are cleaning up all the creativity down to a neat few companies and starting to look at what we are creating as a whole. Our accountants are irreverent and funny, the first year I really started my business I jumped a tax bracket and John called me saying "Do you think you can give us a warning next time?" I promptly told him I planned to earn a minimum the same amount probably in more different currencies!

Accounting should include you and the life you lead running your business. Creative accounting is working the system instead of living within it. There are major advantages you can use to create a better business for yourself from writing off travel as a business expense to minimizing the amount of tax you pay. Be brave, and try diving in – you might even have fun.

You're not wrong, you're not your work, and you're not the source

Nothing you ever do in your life or business is wrong, would you be willing to f*** up? We have all screwed up every now and then, but paralyzing yourself because you 'might" make a mistake or just did make one isn't helping anyone. Like when you fall off a bike or horse, you need to get back on as quickly as possible. Sure take a quick look at what made you fall off, but jump back up as quick as you can.

You are not your work, your business or your job; likewise your business isn't a precious "baby". It wants to take care of itself too. The more you identify you are your job or position the more you lose you – the very creation that made your work happen. What if instead, your work was just one of the things you did or one of the things that makes you money? Sense the lightness in that?

You also don't have to be the sole source of creation for your business – this is for all the control freaks. Yes I mean you!! If you are the only one allowed to contribute to your business how is it ever allowed to expand beyond more than what you alone can create? If you look at the future you can create if you are the lone wolf solely running your business – what does the future look like? Now add 5 staff, 10, 20, or 100! Freak you out a bit? Maybe! But what does that create for the future of your business? That is what you need to start looking for!

Creativity

Is creativity an element you're willing to have in your business or is it relegated to arts, crafts and other artistic pursuits? Business is a very creative occupation if you let it! It's personally one of my favorite sources of creation and if you really go for it the possibilities are infinite.

Have you decided if you are or are definitely not creative? Whatever you have decided here you are correct! I might sound like a broken record if you have read any of my other work with Happy Publishing but I am obsessed with this quote by Gary Douglas:

> "What is creativity? Creativity is the vision of your life and the work that you desire to do as the essence of you, as the soul of energy. Everything that you do, done from the energy of creativity, regardless of whether you are sweeping the floor, cleaning the toilets, washing the windows, washing the dishes, cooking the meal, writing the checks, creates a different possibility and a different result." –

Creativity is not defined from result, from how many ideas you produce in a day or how out of the box your business is – it's a generative energy you add to everything you be, do, create and generate in business and also in your life.

A creative life is an interesting one – one of exploration, possibilities, and things never showing up how you thought it was going to plus more. When you're willing to let yourself go – really truly give yourself the green light to create anything – wonderful, awful, boring, out there or anything in-between the brakes come off. The juices get revving and you can start to go.

How much more would your business expand if you let yourself loose on it? Would you be willing to?

How to have fun

Speaking of something else you might not be willing to have, let's talk about fun in business. Yep I said it FUN and BUSINESS. Can it really go together? Really I think the question is: Are you willing to?

Anything can be fun if you let it, but most people I find would rather revel in the misery of their working life than create a different possibility. Gary Douglas has said over and over "Happiness is just a choice". It's the choice no one really wants to make though!

Having your happiness in your own hands as a choice to have or not requires a sense of bravery and even balls to do it. Do you dare have fun in every area of your life – even the serious parts? Your point of view creates your reality, does the adventure of business surprise and delight you or provide an endless task after task – basically paid slavery to money.

Fun in business isn't laughing hysterically having lots of parties (although in all the businesses I work in we do! Richard Branson is also a strong believer in this). It's about the joy of creation, the fun of making money and working together. Fun can be an ever-present element in your business if you are willing to invite it to be there.

Fun doesn't want to come to the party with no food, bad music and frowning faces. It wants to be part of the exuberance of living.

If your business was a party – would fun be coming to it?

Work with people

I'm not sure how much I can fit in this small segment about this, it could be a book entirely on its own! The incredible skills I have learnt in working with people are my constant companion and favorite tool. The world of business does not go round by machines and systems, it's carried out by people – no matter how wonderful, annoying or in between they are – are you grateful for them?

Practice being grateful for every single person that contributes and interacts with your business, whether they are an integral part or not, paying client or not. Gratitude is a palpable energy that is a greater contribution than anything else for the expansion of your business.

Recognize that everyone is different and has their unique point of view. No two people have the exact same experience, awareness or capacities. So how can you use that to your advantage and empower those you work with to become even greater. Contrary to popular belief, empowering your staff to out create you makes your business better and if you are worried about them leaving then you might want to look at your entire viewpoint of the universe.

There are more than enough talented, capable amazing people on the planet, would it be the end of the world if they left? And are you treating those you work with so well they would never want to? No one wants to stay long term where they feel pinned down or held back. By empowering your staff to be the best they can be you become one of the best people to work with.

Do your staff work with you or for you? If your staff work *for* you, do they ever get to truly be creative, own their work and have their own ideas or does everything fall back on you? If you work *with* people there is a completely different energy and possibility available. Do incredibly talented people want to work for someone or with someone? Are you creating yourself as the leader people would love to create something with? Keep this in mind as you continue creating and adding to your business.

The three elements to making a business work

There are three elements every business needs no matter what industry to truly be successful, and they aren't what you think they might be. Gary Douglas, the founder of Access Consciousness came up with these and every day they turn out to be true. Every business requires the energy of Creator, Connector and Mover in order to thrive.

A Creator is the one who is always coming up with a new generative idea, they would probably die if they didn't come up with a new idea every day. They seldom often get past the idea stage and end up judging themselves as a failure because they didn't have the capacity to "follow through" with their genius creations. Stay tuned because this will become a lot clearer in the next sections.

Connectors seem a bit more obvious – they can talk to anyone. You're looking for someone who can do XYD and your friend's grandma hires one and does a great job! They couldn't go a day without talking to people, they are one of the few people that actually really like people. Connectors however have a hard time getting paid for their capacity at this, or if they do – they don't always like it and start to not like connecting anymore. This isn't a capacity you can force.

Movers have a futurist point of view, a Creator will tell them their idea and then the Movers start looking at what does it actually take to make this a reality – this would need to happen and this obstacle might come up and these future possibilities might appear and we would definitely need to deal with this. They have in innate capacity to know what has to happen when but often judge themselves for not coming up with the idea in the first place.

However all three of these energies of capacities work together brilliantly, a Creator comes up with a great idea, a Mover looks at what it takes to make it a reality and Connector gets it to spread.

Sounds like a fairytale? What if it was truly this easy to expand your business? Now, which one are you? Take a look at what one you find the least and the most valuable out of these three.

I was in Istanbul with Simone Milasas, the founder of Joy of Business and we were having a conversation in the class about these three energies. At lunch I was telling her how frustrated I was that I couldn't get the team I was working with going on what needed to happen next. So she asked me which one of these I found the most valuable and the least. I said "Oh definitely Movers, they are the ones that make everything happen and Creators are the least valuable, all they do is come up with ideas."

Then she asked me what I thought my colleague was who is a Connector, then when she came to lunch, Simone asked her which she thought was the most valuable and least. Her reply was "Oh Creators are the most amazing people, they come up with the brilliant things! Probably for me, the least valuable is connecting" which is exactly what she is!

Then I finally got it, I am a Creator of magnitude and I have been trying to make myself a Mover. You can never truly see what you are naturally being, which is why you find it the least valuable. The thing you find the most valuable is probably not the most natural for you, it doesn't mean you can't do it, just that it's not as natural a capacity as the others.

If you weren't judging you, what capacity are you already being you have not yet acknowledged? And how can you use that to your full advantage? Now the ideas pour out of me and I now ask; "Who is a Mover that can help me make this a reality?"

Different or differently

What is the difference between these two words? Am I being nitpicky or is there something behind this. When you do something differently, essentially you are doing the same thing with a small adjustment. When you do something different you are changing it entirely.

Insanity is doing the same thing over and over again and expecting a different result. If you are only slightly changing something, can you truly expect a drastically different result? Or here's a different question: Are you willing to change absolutely everything if you know it will create something greater?

The great entrepreneurs and creators of the world didn't try to "tweak" the tried and tested, they went out on a limb with sometimes the barest of a hunch to create what they did.

If you let yourself go with your hunches, your knowing, your innate instincts – would you dare to be as different as you truly be? Doing business different as opposed to differently will allow you to be on the creative innovative edge of your industry (or create an entirely new one!!).

The real question is how much are you willing to know? And how much are you willing to go for it?

Change in a nanosecond

One of the biggest dangers I see in business is in doing what has always been done and not recognizing when a change is required. Now, I am definitely not perfect at this and tend to hold onto my preciously created systems, ideas and ways of doing things as much as anyone else in business, I happen to be fortunate enough to work with some of the fastest changing people on the planet though!

If you are too busy holding onto your superior point of view that worked wonderfully (for 10 seconds) is it truly what is going to work for the next 10? Not being too attached to your own ideas and having an interesting, truly inquisitive unfixed point of view about everything is one of the keys to being able to recognize when change is needed.

As soon as something becomes fixated, stuck, stagnant or no longer has that creative energetic life force to it in your business ask yourself; "Does this require changing?"

If you are willing to change anything in a nanosecond, creating a fluid business that can move with an ever-changing time becomes much easier. Kodak for example said that digital film would never take off and people would still like film – now it's becoming a dying company. Change, I think is business's middle name – and besides, isn't it the fun part?

Can you truly say you don't like the thrill of change? This is why lots of businesses rise and fall, because we love starting from scratch. What if instead of letting your businesses fail when you are over it, instead you allowed it to change – every 10 seconds if that's what was required to make it interesting for you. I dare you to do it.

Boredom

Boredom is a sign that it's time for a change in your world. It's an energetic signal that there's a new reality and possibility you haven't chosen yet. Does doing one thing at a time ever truly excite you? Or would having multiple things being created at the same time make your life exciting enough?

You need 10+ things on your plate at all times to truly continue moving forward with your endeavors, otherwise especially in business it feels like everything is going to slow and you start getting in the way of yourself creating extra problems where none truly need to be had. You have a choice to either be OCC – an Obsessive Compulsive Creator or as Gary Douglas calls it an OCCC – an Obsessive Compulsive Creator of Crap!

Which would you rather choose? By adding more to your life you are constantly adding new and fresh energy to all your projects and creations. It keeps things feeling fresh and new.

If you're not sure what to add to your business and life ask yourself one of my favorite questions: What possibilities are available you have not yet instituted?

Keep asking it without any expectation of an answer and be surprised how your life and business shows up.

The Author

Rebecca Hulse

www.CreatingBusinessBeyondThisReality.com/rebecca-hulse

CHAPTER 9

Just Do It Already!

JENNILYNNE COLEY

BUSINESS... that illustrious, multifaceted, and sometimes confusing word.

So, what exactly is business anyway? And what does it mean to you?

Go ahead, take a few minutes and write it down.

_____

_____

_____

_____

_____

_____

_____

_____

_____

_____

According to Merriam Webster's Dictionary, business is the activity of making, buying, or selling goods or providing services in exchange for money; work that is part of a job; the amount of activity that is done by a store, company, factory, etc.

Is that what you wrote down? My guess is that was not exactly the first thing that came to mind for you.

Or what about the revered finance resource Investopedia? Curious what they had to say about business??? Their definition is as follows: A business is an organization or enterprising entity engaged in commercial, industrial or professional activities. A company transacts business activities through the production of a good, offering of a service or retailing of already manufactured products.

Was that a little closer to what you wrote? Perhaps it was, and maybe it was not...

So, what's my point here? Well, you can look at a number of different "sources" and you will find different definitions of the word business. And to look at the idea of creating business beyond this reality, doesn't it make sense to first start with a "common" definition of business? Deductive reasoning says so as that's precisely what we're taught to do as we enter school, the corporate world, and even the land of entrepreneurship. It's supposed to be a constant process of elimination and calculating, measuring sticks, targets, and figuring out the right answer in order to be considered "successful"....most of it involving judging against some preconceived and commonly agreed upon set of standards, ideas or definitions. And while that has its place in certain situations and circumstances, has it ever really, truly worked for you?

Let's go on a little journey together...back to around the year 1994. I was eleven years old, and I was a dreamer. I had pages and pages written down of all the things I would someday accomplish. Things like owning my own amusement park, teen girls' center, homeless shelter, clothing line, you name it! I just knew that I could and would do it ALL! And that summer, I had started to set the wheels in motion for my very own t-shirt line. My sister and I spent our entire summer taking pretend phone calls for pretend orders on a very real phone, with real lunch breaks, selling our pages of designs for our t-shirt line we had drawn up all the designs for.

We had so much fun, not thinking for one moment we couldn't or wouldn't be "successful". We even pitched the idea to our grandpa who politely turned down our solicitation for his investment in turning our imaginary business into a reality. And while it really hurt at the time, and somewhat even crushed our dreams, there was a massive huge gift in that experience. You see it's really easy to keep going when you're "winning" and things are going your way. And unfortunately, that is not the reality of life. There will be valleys... you will "fail"... everything will not be perfect. And while you can have a sense of peace no matter what shows up if you choose to, the dips in the roller coaster called life are a necessary part of the experience just like the inclines...and the dips can become smaller as you grow and evolve. The key is in being like a rocket ship when it's on its way to outer space. Did you know that it is actually off course 99.9% of the time, yet it still manages to reach its destination by making little tiny course corrections? So instead of judging your "mistakes" and calling them failures, be more like a rocket ship. Don't make it significant or meaningful. Instead keep going, keep choosing and keep creating... course correct.

One of the other lessons I learned from being "rejected" was that your friends and family are not your marketing or sales force and they may or may not become your customers. No one will love your vision as much as you do. Please don't make this meaningful about you or them in any way. Some of them may choose not to support you for various reasons, maybe because they're afraid you will leave them behind, or perhaps it strikes a nerve in the part of them that's afraid to create what they know is possible, and maybe they just don't know the best way to help or support you. None of it really matters because while they can and may help get the word out, they are not your source to rely on. There's a reason that very well-known multi-million and billion dollar brands still have massive marketing budgets, even paying millions for one 30–60 second spotlight commercial during the Super Bowl. That being said, how can you stay top of mind for your target audience? A great thing about social media and technology is you can have your very own television station for little or no cost and you control the programming. So, what kind of content would you like to share with the world? And how can you use this messaging to effectively and profitably grow your brand?

Back to this idea about traditional business... do you avoid it like the plague or use it as the measurement tool of judgement for success or failure? What are the valuable gifts we can receive from this traditional model or idea?

One possibility is looking at the different types of entities that can be run in different ways... C-Corp, S-Corp, LLC, partnership, etc. Do you know what those are, and what the advantages and disadvantages are from a structural and tax perspective? Just a little food for thought as the point isn't to give you any sort of explanation or advice. The bigger question is what if you actually ran your entire life like a well-run, thriving corporation? What if you could take your emotions and feelings out of the equation and begin to run your life from an objective birds-eye level view... truly willing to look at what is working and what isn't working and be willing to make adjustments accordingly at both regular and irregular intervals. After all, aren't checkups important? You have annual exams at the doctor to check your health, biannual, or even quarterly dental cleanings, depending on the health of your teeth and gums, report cards in school, and annual reviews at a job. And while most of those are used as judgment tools, what if you could use them to assist you with your course corrections for the rocket ship of your business and life?

So, are you willing to be the CEO, COO & CFO of the business of your life?

As the CEO of your life, you take a birds-eye of view of the health and wellness of the creation of your life with regular checkups daily, weekly, monthly, quarterly and annually... or at whatever other intervals you see fit... maybe it's more irregular when you get an awareness that it's time to take inventory. Whatever your method, this allows you to gauge whether you are on track or off track to hitting your targets and then ask what else you could add or change to get closer to achieving them. You're driving yourself, and everyone else who's contributing to stay committed to you, your vision and your mission for your reality, business and life.

As the COO, you're looking at how you're actually running your day-to-day operations and how that's working for you. Do you maybe require a different system or strategy? Are there people you can add to your life that can help you create your targets? How are you communicating your vision out into the world and how is it all working together for you? The chore chart, the daily routine with going for a run, meditating, writing gratitude notes, watching television, getting the kids to/ from school and extracurricular activities... how does this all work as smoothly as possible so that when it all hits the fan, and it always does in life, the bumps are more like little speed bumps than entire mountains to climb that stop you in your tracks?

As the CFO, you're in tune with how your financial literacy, or lack thereof is contributing to the creation of your life. Are you keeping a personal balance sheet, income statement and cash flow statement? Are you crystal clear on what's coming in and what's going out? Just like a company requires capital and reserves to run efficiently and remain in business over time, the overall creation of your life does as well, especially if you would like to thrive instead of survive. Money is required if you'd actually like to have the kind of life that lights you up and to be able to create the possibilities in the world that only you can create. Businesses require capital to run and reserves for the up and down roller coaster of incoming revenue streams. Most businesses fail because they run out of capital long before they have an opportunity to weather the storm to success; this same concept applies in bankruptcy situations. So, do you truly understand how money works and how it can literally be working for you instead of you working for it? To increase your financial IQ, you can take classes, study online resources, read books, and even hire people to assist you in this area such as accountants,

CPAs, financial planners, etc. What can be even more empowering is to have a certain level of awareness around all of this, especially when it comes to knowing who to hire and how well they're actually working for you.

How do you create money and allow it to contribute to you in such a way that when you hit those speed bumps, money isn't the excuse or the problem that you also have to solve in the midst of it all? How much peace are you willing to have around money such that it doesn't become the deciding factor for your choices? Doing so allows you to take the emotion out of what's showing up or not showing up and what you've created or haven't created versus your actual targets. Without getting caught up in emotions, you can have more clarity and greater results. Isn't that what we're all after? Reaching our goals? Creating a life we love to live? Emotions can be incredibly distracting and actually hinder us in doing so.

Now let's talk a little more specifically about business and the creation of it in the traditional sense. Maybe you've been in business for a long time, maybe you're new in business and just getting started, or maybe you have an idea and haven't yet had the courage to pull the trigger and get going. Wherever you're at, it can create so much more to act like you're just getting started, excited, curious, willing to learn and grow and adjust to whatever will actually work for the business.

If you're still in the idea stage and haven't gotten started yet, my question for you is why not? Now I know what it's likes to have an idea and not be willing to pull the trigger. Just a few years ago, I was working at a job that I was really good at, yet I was putting in a lot of hours and I wasn't really sure how to fit in a business as a single mom of very active children in sports. I knew I wanted to work for myself, and I also knew I had to pay bills. With all of the extra hours I was putting in, how on earth was I going to run a company? Now I had taken some certification courses for the business I have now and yet I was too scared to take the leap and walk away to get it up and running. I knew I had a calling to move on, and I desired to. I was asking lots of questions and looking at how it could possibly work, and then one day on my way to work...it happened. I was rear ended by a woman who wasn't paying attention as we were stopping at a red light, and a few days later a concussion diagnosis occurred that prevented me from returning to work anyway.

When we don't listen to the whispers of the Universe, the gentle nudges go from subtle to very loud like being hit upside the head with a two-by-four. Please do not wait until you're whacked upside the head figuratively or literally to act on what you already know. I spent a few months recovering and in that recovery time, my practice went from just an idea that I might get to someday, to a love I was finally willing to explore, contribute to and allow to contribute to me. For the first year, I ran it out of my house, and then I got an office space. Moving to an office space was a scary next move, and it was just what the business needed and was asking for. There was a lot of trial and error, success and failure or learning of new information/ adjustments, and overall it has added so much to my life and to the lives of my clients, some of which have become great friends.

As you move forward toward the creation of what you know is possible, I'd like to offer a few things to consider. I have some favorite questions I like to ask when interviewing a potential employer or contract offering, and I'm going to apply it here for you. I usually ask, what do you love best and least about working here, and what do you wish you would've known before you started working here? Rarely when I asked those questions did I actually get honest answers. So, I'm going to do my best to give you what I wished I would've known before getting into business.

What do I love best?

For me nothing can replace having control over my time and how I structure my day... being there for my kids when they have important activities/ events. I love the adventure, excitement of the creation of it all. No one dictates a cap on how much I'm paid, and there are many advantages written into the current tax code for businesses.

What do I like least?

It's a constant balance/ dance of personal needs, business needs and providing myself and the business enough space for comfort and ease to grow and expand without any pressure. When I haven't been prepared financially, I've had to borrow money from family/ friends or take side jobs/ contracts to help keep me afloat... not fun and part of being willing to do whatever it takes.

What do I wish I would've known beforehand?

- Cash reserves are critical. If possible, have some sort of "safety net"... savings of 6–12 months, a spouse that can cover your household bills/ expenses, a recurring income stream like an annuity, rental property income, a successful network marketing endeavor, affiliate income...something that is already in place to take the pressure off of you and the business and allow for some creative energy, space and expansion.

- It's all-in, and I mean all-in if you would actually like to succeed.

- Business plans don't actually work, although they can be great guides/ measuring tools to see if you're off track or on track, and sometimes are required by banks/ financial institutions to see if you qualify for a loan.

- It's important to balance and stay off the emotional roller coaster. There will be ups and downs...and the downs will come back up as long as you're willing to follow your awareness and course correct quickly, especially before you run out of money.

- Have as many streams of revenue as you possibly can. The average millionaire has at least seven.

- It's important to partner/ align with influential people who can help refer you and spread the word about your business quickly, help you get clients, and even be great for masterminds. Word of mouth or referral marketing is an excellent long-term strategy to grow a business.

- Success has nothing to do with how smart you are. Align yourself with smart people who know how to access the right resources.

- Tenacity and drive go a long way. Don't quit, especially on a bad day.

- Be true to you who you are and have as much fun as you possibly can along the way. No one, and I mean no one knows more about you, your business and your life than you.

The Author

Jennilynne Coley

www.CreatingBusinessBeyondThisReality.com/jennilynne-coley

CHAPTER 10

Shoe Business

NATALIE KRISHNA

I guess you can say I've created business since I was quite young I would go door to door asking people if I could rake their leaves or shovel snow, babysit, walk their dog anything. I would even clean their houses and I would be paid in many ways sometimes I would get a couple dollars others times I would be paid in books. It didn't matter, I just loved whatever it was I was doing, it was easy for me and I loved making a difference in people's lives. I was young but I saw it created a lot of ease for them. And when I would get paid it was a total bonus.

I have managed to always only do things I loved and was interested in. I never really had a job I hated. It was always something I believe in or adored. For years I've created my life and career following that. (Just things that lit me up) Getting out of high school l knew I wanted to help women and children. I wanted them to feel absolute joy, beautiful, confident and do what they loved. I knew that a women feeling her best would make a difference in the world just by choosing joy and would also spread their light wherever they go. You know the woman one that walks into a room and all eyes are on her. Her smile and joy lights up the room, her laugh is contagious, you can't help but want to be near her know more about her. You just want that in your world

It all started right out of high school I was working in a jewelry section of Our new Walmart that had just opened up. One of the job requirements was to be dressed up and well.... lady like. The manager was a gorgeous confident "independent woman" I loved it. I loved everything she was being. I wanted that. I started taking pride in taking care of myself. I had confidence I got to dress up, wear makeup, and do my nails. I felt good about myself and I wanted other people to feel that.

When I was being brought up the woman in my life were not choosing to dress up or wear makeup. My mother always said natural beauty is better, don't wear makeup it was beaten into me. (Not physically ha-ha but just when I would see a beautiful woman walking that radiated I was drawn to her. and I was immediately shot down just for looking and admiring her. I would hear the woman in my life talking. Look at her thinking she's so damn good all dressed up. So I was taught it was wrong. I also noticed the women in my life would praise one another for anything. It was like no one could do better and if they were rising in some way they would have to be shot down. All of that didn't stop me from loving and adoring the beauty I would see in people and the world. As you could probably tell I was the "black sheep" of the family.

When I was 17 it was just me and my daughter living in our own apartment and I wanted my daughter to have an awesome life so right out of high school I started taking aesthetician courses so I could bring in money doing nails, waxing, manicures, facials etc. This was one of the things that made me feel good and I thought this was a good first step. I would take course at time and build see clients take care of my daughter and go to school for Child and youth care. I didn't want to just help people feel pretty I wanted to help on the inside. Once I was done school I started a part time job working with Teen prostates who didn't really know they were doing it. They were enticed by uncles to do sexual favors in exchange for clothes and food. They didn't really know what they were doing. They just thought it was normal. I didn't last long in that job because from personal experience of my upbringing I had seen several sexual assault psychiatrists and counselors and I hated the way they saw me. It was like I was this victim that would never amount to anything. It was like little and lack was just expected of me. Like yey, look you're not a drug addict or alcoholic bonus for you. The expectations were just so low. and I found the same In the work I was doing so I asked for guidance I would pray and ask where Universe/God whatever you want to call it would have me go and I would follow whatever whispers I would get.

So I started seeing Reiki, and getting drawn to energy work I didn't really know a lot about it but once I started I realized It was something I had been tapped into and following all my life. Like when I was younger on all my adventures alone I would be talking to plants, rocks and animals. Knowing they had a spirit/energy even though I was considered weird. But once I realized it and acknowledged my capacities with energies it opened up new possibilities. I would take the courses work with clients in the spa that I was working at. It started with Reiki I wasn't totally sure people would expect this "out there" thing. This was back in the early 2000s when it wasn't really known yet. But clients I had would try it that led me to more modalities like Massage therapy, Reflexology, aromatherapy, crystal therapy. I followed it all and would mediate and would ask before each client to be a clear energetic channel for them and would follow whatever guidance I would receive. It was amazing. I got guidance to climb sacred mountains with a medicine woman who searched me out and told me I was to work with the next generation of people. I met monks that worked with the Dalai Lama and meditated with them. I went to ceremony shamans. Learned so many things what herbs to use with what. My schedule started filling more and more and while I was working at the spa. One of the local doctors had heard of my results and wanted to know more. We met and chatted we became friends and he invited me in to work with him. I was so scared thinking how on earth I could work with him I didn't know the language the work he was doing. He was so amazing spending time teaching me things, bringing me books inviting me to different conferences. We would see clients together and he would teach me things and I would share with him how I saw things in their bodies, eventually that led me to wanting to learn more and I went to school for Chinese medicine and to Becoming a Holistic Health Practitioner and I didn't even really know what these things where I would learn or what it was. But I knew to follow it.

I ended up becoming so busy with my sessions which we were normalized by saying reiki or massage therapy was just a normal way to invite people into the sessions they didn't fully understand it but loved the benefits and I was incorporating everything I had learned. Each client's session looked totally different. Some people were coming for physical pain some were emotional and what I had found was most of the people it all started with emotional first which would eventually manifest as physical pain in the body. I was noticing after a few months together people had totally transformed. One of my favorite clients had come in and my first time meeting her she walked in she was early 40s head down, she could barely look up and look at me in the eye. It was like she was beaten down. We started off with massage therapy, fire cupping and energy work at the end and she started asking for more energy work, as weeks had gone by. She started talking about and releasing some stuff from her past. Some sexual abuse that had happened that had made her feel trapped and not able to open up. It was like a cycle of no confidence and went into bad relationships with men. She started blossoming more and more over the months we worked together by the end we were just doing energy work and clearing energy blocks by talking. 6 months had gone by and she was a new women she had Confidence she had pep in her step she was dressing up taking care of herself. Our last session together she just cried and shared that she was finally the woman she always dreamed of and wanted to be. Her work changed, her life with her husband was so much more intimate and she started traveling the world like she had always wanted. She was just so vibrant and THAT is what is what I always knew was possible!

I knew we didn't have to be stuck or a victim of our circumstances and that's what I want to do with my life. We didn't have to choose the stigma from abusive pasts or relationships or families. There is this beautiful gem inside of us, just wanting to be free the real us. The one you catch glimpses of when you least expect it the one when you are alone and dancing and it slowly rises and you dance from your soul or your walking in nature and your just being. I loved the blossoming I see in all the people I work with, when they start Discovering more and more of them and what brings them joy. And see that is actually their natural state. When they are feeling contracted and icky it's usually because they are buying other people's stuff and trying to make it real in their world.

For example, me I was always a people pleaser, I just wanted people to like me it didn't matter what it was I had to do I would see what it was, and become that in exchange for them to like me. It wasn't my brightest moment. BUT what I discovered the more energetically aware I became if I did that my body would feel icky I would start feeling crappy so I saw it was my bodies way of telling me "Hey, this doesn't work you're going to create more poo if you go down this road" So now I know to stop but before I would just keep going with it and Yes it would always create a bunch of crap in my life. We learn this from such a young age, how we are supposed to be what "good little girls and boys do" and if you don't follow that well you're bad and wrong. So like good little kids we either comply and listen to our parents or resist but either way that slowly chips away at our spirit. I want to bring out the Real you, the you that was taught to hideaway or shrink.

I wanted to invite people to other possibilities eventually my hands-on sessions morphed into possibilities sessions where I realized I was able to work with people from all over the world on the phone. We would work in different areas of their life. We look at what they are wanting to create and all of the blocks that are holding them back. We remove those and choose beyond it. I'm so grateful I've always listened to the whispers of the universe its opened doorways and new possibilities that hadn't existed before in mine and all the people I work with lives. Something they had been stuck on just disappears and new things become possible. All my careers had never existed before I saw a different possibility available in the world and I followed the lightness on how to create it. I didn't know what it would look like but I trusted my knowing. To this day I continue to study things that add to me and my client's life. I never know what that is going to be but I know when I'm drawn to it, it eventually pops up or the information is required in a session I'm having with a client. I love that we co create together the life they want. Well really it's them choosing it I just get to facilitate the process. I find my clients create that too. They ask for what they want or we look at what they want to change or create and while we remove any blocks the universe rearranges things so they become a possibility.

One of the biggest things I›ve learned on this journey is The Universe has your back, when you ask and are open to receive your ask becomes a morphing possibility on the planet.

Follow your bliss and the Universe will open doors where there were only walls ~Joseph Campbell

The Author

Natalie Krishna

www.CreatingBusinessBeyondThisReality.com/natalie-krishna

CHAPTER 11

Business Done Differently

DONNA MARTUGE

If someone told me ten years ago I would write about business, wealth and success I would have laughed heartily. I was always good at creating money. However, business is something I told myself I could NOT do. I always said, "I don't know how to own or run a business"

I am not sure where that belief came from, and the point of creation is irrelevant.

Once I became aware of this belief I had, I had to consciously choose to change it if I was going to choose to own a business. Thankfully, changing thought patterns and processes is definitely an area of expertise for me, and I use that to my advantage. First, of course you must become aware of the beliefs that are limiting you and/or choose the beliefs that will support you in what you desire to create. Although this chapter is not about thoughts and beliefs specifically, you will see the connection between your thoughts and beliefs and your ability to create and sustain an extraordinary business.

The goal of this chapter is for you to be able to walk away after reading it and immediately take one or more actions that you learned from it that can change your business now. I would like to share with you what I learned in the process of creating my businesses and from my experience coaching business owners, so you too can create and expand a business in this fast paced business world that will last the test of time. The life cycle of businesses is quickly getting shorter. Today 90 percent of businesses close within the first five years. I have been lucky enough to have worked with thousands of people across 10 or so countries. When you work with people for as long as I have, the way that I do, you begin to see patterns. In patterns there is a wealth of information you can use to your advantage. I am excited to share some of that information with you, information you generally do not get in business school.

I am far from the expert in the field of business, my area of expertise is in the field of creating a coaching business, however I have worked with many businesses and business owners and coached them to success. There are key factors to creating and sustaining a successful business. I have taken 5 Keys out of my Business Success Program to share with you here in this chapter.

DECISIONS IN EACH MOMENT

The first key is to be aware of the decisions you make in every moment. Anthony Robbins teaches people that we make 3 decisions in every moment that shape our lives. As someone who loves, knows and believes that our thoughts at this moment create our future, I personally see this as an important key to creating any success in your life. It is amazing to realize we actually do make many decisions in every moment. I am going to break that down in parts so it is easy to see.

The first decision we make is what we are going to focus on. From the moment we wake up in the morning we are constantly choosing what we will focus on right at this moment. Often this may be an automatic like a habit that has developed over time. The more you are willing to be conscious of your thoughts and focus the more you can control the next two decisions.

The exact moment we choose a focus, we make our second decision. We give that focus a meaning. The meaning you choose to give your focus is a choice and a decision. We often do not see that the meaning we give something is a choice. However, you can see the choice when you look at situations that many people face and see the differences in their reaction and description. For example; two people may both be going through a divorce. One may describe the divorce as an ending. They may believe they lost their one and only soul mate and they will never fall in love again. Another person may describe their divorce as a new beginning. A chance to meet someone and have a relationship greater than any relationship they have ever known. Both people are going through a divorce and both give their situations very different meanings. The meaning you give the point of focus is important, it then leads to your emotional state.

The emotional state we are in drives our actions. How many times in your life have you planned a conversation with someone very carefully, possibly even rehearsed it in your mind and then when you go and have the conversation it happens completely different than you had planned? You walk away, shake your head as you say to yourself "That is not when I wanted to say". This could be because you were frustrated, and said words you did not mean. You may have been in a great mood and said yes to something you practiced saying no to. The emotional state we choose drives our actions.

How many points in your life can you identify where you can say if you made a different choice, you would have a different life? The three decisions we make in every moment shapes our future. We can all identify specific decisions that we know led us on one path versus another possible path.The important piece of information here is, as you become more aware of your thoughts and focus, you begin to make more conscious choices in these moments. You learn from practice, truly like building any muscle, how to choose your focus and meaning, and how to create the emotional state you desire to have every day. You can choose to deliberately create your future now.

DRIVING FORCES

There are driving forces related to everything we do in life. The one we will look at here is your target. What is your target for your business? What is motivating you? What would you like to create? Many people begin their businesses without getting really clear on what their vision is for their business now and in the future. Knowing your vision and being connected to it is truly what has helped many companies remain at the top of their industry in recent years. If you look at some of the leading companies that have been around a long time and exist today, you can see points where they needed to look at their companies, realign with their vision, and strategically be innovative to regain ground and get ahead of their competition.

Nike is an excellent example. Phil Knight began his business selling other peoples product. Being an athlete himself, he had an interest in great products for athletes. He had found a company in Japan that made a running shoe he loved at a low cost and he signed a contract to bring that running shoe to the United States. His vision was truly about bringing great products to athletes.

After some time the company had decided to end their contract with Phil Knight. Knight was faced with either closing down his business or finding a way to out create what he had done thus far. He used his vision to keep him focused. What do athletes require? What am I creating that athletes need and that adds value to their lives? These are questions your vision will answer. These questions led Phil Knight from selling someone else's product to creating a product that represented a lifestyle.

Today Nike is a brand. When you think of Nike you think "Just Do It". You connect those words to sneakers, clothes and now that has expanded to a whole community. You can go online in the Nike community and find a running group, tennis group or any sport near you that you can join. In November of 2015 Forbes named Knight the 15th richest person in the world with an estimated net worth of 28. 1 billion dollars. Today he owns other companies such as the stop motion film company Laika and he is a philanthropist. He turned what someone may have perceived as an ending into a beginning. He used his vision to create a phenomenal company that is sustainable over time.

It is important to note, his vision was not connected to sales. This is not to say you should not focus on money. You cannot survive in business if you're not making money. However, if you are going to focus on a sale as a main target, you will not be able to survive in business through the years. Your vision is connected to your target of what you want to create and contribute. It is connected to adding value somehow in your clients/customers lives. If you focus on a sale you can sell a product to a customer who buys from you once and never returns. If you focus on value and contribution, you create raving fans that stay loyal and follow you through the years.

ANTICIPATION and STRATEGIC INNOVATION

When you look at businesses all over the world you can see that often businesses fail because they do not anticipate what is coming. If you are leading a business/organization/company and you are not anticipating what is coming then you are leading from reaction. This means that businesses often fail because of the leaders or owners skills and mindset. The question becomes how do you lead from anticipation? Obviously we can't predict the future. However, you can be ahead of the game if you anticipate that you will need to continually shift and strategically innovate.

Leading a business is fluid and ever changing. In the past many businesses set up structures, created a product or a service, advertised and marketed, and were able to stay in business for a long period of time. Today the life span of a product or service can be as short as 6 months to a year. A successful business must make it part of their plan to have scheduled improvements each year.

Improvements may be the look of your product, or an improvement that adds value to your customers/clients, or both. In the 1980's Sony was a leader in the field of electronics. At that time they were innovative. If you are my age you may remember in the 1980's there seemed to be a "bigger is better" perception. Companies were creating boom boxes and big stereo systems. However, Sony looked at what people needed and valued. They realized people travel more and were much more mobile. At a time that everyone was making radios bigger, Sony came out with the Walkman. This helped them get the edge in the market at that time. An edge that today *Apple Incorporated* currently holds.

Apple began in 1976 and became the leader in the field of technology. Today it is the world's largest information technology company as far as revenue. In November of 2014 Apple became the first United States company to be valued at $700 billion dollars. The company is known for staying connected to it's vision, for consistently, at least once a year, making product updates and new products that are easy to use and fulfill clients needs. You can certainly see that they have created the raving fan base that I refer to earlier, that makes business sustainable over time. They do this by anticipating needs and values and committing to continually improve their products adding more value for their customers.

Although Apple Incorporated cannot predict what the future needs will be, their commitment to focusing on constant improvement, value and knowing their clients needs, even needs their clients may not know they have, has created a company that is designed to stay on the leading edge of success over time.

QUESTIONS

The quality of the information you get about business or anything in life is a result of the quality of your question. Are you asking questions that will create the outcome you desire? Most people ask questions that have a presupposition built in them. Everyone has at least one primary question they are always asking, often unconsciously.

Often it is the type of question that is not a question at all, it is a conclusion and a judgement spoken like a question. For example, a common question I hear from some clients is "why do I always fail?" Or " how can I make everyone happy?". These questions lead to circular thinking and no real answer or helpful information. They keep us "stuck" in the same situation we have seen before.

As a business owner and leader you want to ask questions that open up doorways of possibility. Bill Gates has a question that drove Microsoft. It was a question he asked and he expected everyone that worked with him and for him to ask. He asked, "How can I become the intelligence that runs all the computers around the world?" He came up with the idea of developing a common software system. He asked an effective question and the answer placed him on the leading edge of computer software around the world.

Questions you may want to ask are, "who is our customer and who do we want our customers to be?", "where can I get a new perspective?", What distribution channels and resources are available that I am not currently using?". There are hundreds of effective questions you can ask, and it is worth your time to sit and write some down.

Peter Drucker said, "my greatest strength as a consultant is to be ignorant and ask a few questions". His suggestions for questions were often simple and quite profound. For example, he once asked Jack Welch when he was working as a consultant for General Electric "if you weren't already in this business would you enter it today? and if the answer is no what are you going to do about it?". (Drucker Institute). These questions helped Welch look at General Electric and realign his resources and focus, which shifted the company in a good way. Effective questions are one of the greatest tools you can use in every area of your life.

RESOURCEFULNESS

Earlier I stated that the majority of new businesses fail in the first five years of opening. When you speak to business owners they have a list of reasons why they think they failed. Some mention money, time, skills, they may say they did not know the right people, or it was the timing. Research will show you that none of those reasons are accurate. Think about it, we have billion dollars companies that were created by people who had no resources. We have people who have every resource at their disposal unable to maintain a job or a relationship. Resources is never the answer to success or failure. It is your willingness to be resourceful.

One of the first business I ever created was a publishing company. I had no idea, or at least I thought I had no idea how to open a publishing company. I did not know the details involved and it is not what I went to school for, even though as a teenager I used to dream about opening a publishing company. I was inspired by Louise Hay and all that she created in her life and the world.

Ironically, I did not plan on opening a publishing company. I received a call from someone who had a vision for a publishing company but did not have the time, nor the desire to focus on the details of creating it or running it. When I received the call I literally felt a joy in my body and my soul that led me to the memory of my teenage dream and my gut feeling was, 'say yes'. Thankfully I did say yes and I laid the groundwork and set up the structures, relationships, employees, services and everything else required for Access Consciousness Publishing Company. The fact that I was creating this for a company whose vision is "empowering people to know what they know" was in alignment with everything I love, empowering others and helping them get where they want to go. Once I said yes, I had a lot to learn very quickly. It was at this moment when all of my thoughts about what business is, how it is created and done every day, and all the skills I believed I had and did not have came up. Some of those thoughts helped me, and other thoughts could have stopped me in my tracks if I let them. I had to be resourceful to create this company.

Now not only did I have to change my beliefs about whether I could do business or not, I also had to look at my definitions of what business looks like and how it is structured to create the foundation of the company. One of the first tasks was figuring out where to start as the company was going to have two home bases, one in California and one in Australia, and at the time I was living in New York. Today business is so different. I had to think different. I had to think globally and virtually. This company was not going to be an office building where people come into an office every day and work in the same space. This company as it was envisioned by the owners required the ability to have employees all over the world, that worked in their own homes or offices and met regularly in a virtual meeting space. A company that runs 24 hours a day because we have employees in countries all over the world, and in different time zones. I had to be resourceful to create the company.

Resourcefulness is determination, creativity, effective questions, curiosity and wonder. It is the willingness to let go of every definition and conclusion you have ever known and go beyond those boundaries. Truthfully every belief and definition I had related to what business was, I had to let go and ask questions. It was one of the greatest experiences of my life. From there I created my greatest business thus far, Beyond A Moment in Time which continues to expand.

There are so many amazing keys to share about creating a successful and sustainable business. Remember, you do not need to know everything. Be resourceful, stay in question and get a coach. The average return on investment in a coach is 700 percent. The business world changes quickly and it can work to your advantage to have people available to you who already have the skills and expertise in areas that you may require it, use them.

Incorporating some of the keys in this chapter can help you not only achieve success, but also feel fulfilled, and that my friend is part of phenomenal living.

The Author

Donna Martuge

www.CreatingBusinessBeyondThisReality.com/donna-martuge

CHAPTER 12

Uncovering Business Possibilities Previously Hidden from My Reality

KRISTEN TRIMMER

I have been in business for myself for over 10 years running a day spa and wellness center and with this have had many peaks and valleys of huge success and epic failures. I will be the first to tell you that I have not always or frequently been what is considered joyful with business-or created beyond this reality with my business. In fact, I would tell you that there have been many moments and probably more moments than not, when I have been the exact opposite of joy in my business. I sometimes have hated being in business for myself. I have been forceful, aggressive and destructive to get stuff done inside my enterprise.

While this energy is necessary at times, I know that there is an easier way to be with business. Sometimes I wish that I knew earlier in my business, what I know now. I also am now aware in writing this how much I will choose to have a different possibility in my business of play and ease and abundance. As this has not always been my first choice previously-but it will be now. I am not saying I have any regrets, as I know that it is all a process and I have been a part of an amazing journey to get to where I am now. However, what I would wish for with anyone who chooses to read this book is for YOU after reading this book to have more of an awareness of your capabilities on being joyful in business, right away. I would like for you to have the possibility to have more ease in your business faster than I chose to for myself. It is possible to do create this for yourself however, it is simply a choice. Will you make that choice for yourself?

When wondering what to write for this chapter I am aware of all the funny limitations I posed on myself that are untrue throughout the years. For me when going through this chapter it is almost as if I was going back 10 years ago to tell myself what I wish I knew earlier to make it easier for me in running my business. This is also what I have noticed in colleagues and in other businesses their limitations that have come up that are not true and can easily be navigated through. Especially if you don't buy the lies of these – and are honest with yourself in what you would like to create. These are the lies of the business world otherwise known as this reality and if you can create beyond them you will be amazed at the different possibilities that will show up for you. In the business world in this reality you will come up with many different limits people impose upon themselves and the business world. All of which are lies or can be lies if you choose differently. Most people don't always perceive business as being easy or fun. You can choose differently if you would like to, though.

Recently I was at a home improvement store and it was near Halloween time. My 2-year-old son and I happened to come up near a display with 6-foot-tall goblins, monsters, witches and a pretty gory, gruesome scene. Now I knew this wasn't real however, for my son thought this was very real. I found myself as he bolted from my hand running down the aisles screaming and I was chasing him yelling "Colin it is ok" "It is not real; the monsters are not real" I know this may seem like it has nothing to do with what I am talking about right now. But what I would like to ask you is how many times do we make our limitations "monsters" and we run away screaming instead of facing them, recognizing that it is not real and a lie and move forward towards our targets with what we would like to create and to succeed? Aren't limitations self-imposed? Do we when we come up against something that is scary believe they are monsters, when in fact it is nothing but a façade? If we made ourselves truly get this can you imagine how much simpler everything would be in business?

I am experienced in buying the lies of this world and in business. But when you start to choose differently for yourself and create what you desire regardless of what is going on with anyone else, everything becomes much easier. One of the first lies of this reality I have come up against is don't buy that you need a college degree or any certification to be in business for yourself in any regards to do well. Some of the people I have seen do well in business have rarely had a degree. It's funny as I have my business degree, but I in no way shape or form feel it helped me do better than anyone else. Maybe in some ways it made me look better to people or they judged that I was smarter because I had a degree, but it didn't teach me much. Sure, I could read the books and be tested on the material like anyone else but I still had to learn hands on just as much as anyone else who would be in business for themselves. I needed to be willing to be the energy of what was needed and put forth the effort to easily find what I desired to make my business work. It is being committed to doing well for yourself. It is making the choice to succeed, regardless of what shows up. How many times do businesses fail as the people running them are not willing to push forward and let themselves succeed? How many times do you resist the push forward and say no instead of saying yes to achieving what you would like? How many times have you let yourself believe you needed to finish or complete something else before you could do what you wanted to do? What are the excuses you made about what you had to finish first before you could start your new creation? Look at this... is it even true or do you need to do this? Like completing a degree or finishing that certification? Do you know all of this is a lie?

Most people who do well in business it is because they commit to doing well. I know that I had that part down-I would succeed regardless. Here is the funny thing though the business degree did not help me in the slightest. If anything from my perspective, I may have wasted a bit of time. I don't regret getting my business degree or going to college there are advantages to it. I have a young son and I would encourage him to consider if nothing else than to have the experience and completing the degree. Having a degree may give you more options-and more options is nice. I just know that I could have done what I am doing now without a degree. So please the next time you find yourself thinking you need to know more to do anything let it go and do what you would like. Just allow yourself to step into the energy of doing what you would like to make your business succeed and yourself succeed.

If you want to be an entrepreneur or you are already an entrepreneur what you truly are is a creator. They should have degrees for that. I am a creator. A creator of everything, a creator of all. Think how excited you get when you create something. You know this is what you are good at if you are an entrepreneur, correct? Have you ever acknowledged that? Most entrepreneurs can be jack of all trades master of none. What if you don't make yourself wrong for this? As a kid, I would take dance classes, gymnastics, and sign language classes and then I would learn a lot get bored and most times not want to advance any further. Is that wrong? Or are we allowed to have some interest in something for as long as needed and then move on? Isn't this a strength that we can be involved in more than one activity at once and learn as much as we want and then learn more about something else?

When you first start your business and when you know what you would you would like your business to be, make sure you create a business plan just for yourself. But I don't mean the typical business plan-be honestly clear with what you would like to create in your business for yourself-every detail-and make this fun and playful. Not anyone else's idea of what your business should be like but what it will be like for you and what you desire. Make this fun it doesn't need to be tedious. I would ask yourself: What kind of hours do you want to work? Do you want to work from home? What amount of money do you want to make? What limitations do you have for yourself-which are untrue? Do you like working with other people? Do you like working by yourself? What do you like to do in the business? What do you sometimes need more help with? Would it be easier to work while you create your new business somewhere else so you have additional income coming in? Is it easier to let someone else do an aspect of your business that you don't like to do? What amount of money do you need to make to live off? Be detailed and very clear in what you would like to create for yourself in your life and with your business. But ask yourself what you would like to create in your life mostly. Be aware that you are still going to have to do quite a bit and be committed to changing targets and goals but to do whatever it takes to get there.

Sometimes I have found that people will create an idea for a business but then not actually DO anything about it. You can create all day-but if you don't institute a strategy and move forward with it and act on it you most likely you will not become a successful business. In this reality, there is structure and form to business. Use this to your advantage. Don't stop, continue to move forward or you may not succeed. It's that simple. Don't stop-keep on moving. But how many people stop? When you are about to stop is then when you are about to succeed greater than you perceived possible? To have fun doing what you love makes this so much more joyful. What if money follows you when you are happier?

Business can be ease and playful if you are honest with yourself and what you would like to create within your business. If what you are creating isn't easy or fun for you there will be a barrier up and it may be difficult to generate money, business and creating a new way of doing business beyond this reality. Also, pay attention to things you are in resistance to being in your business. Like for example for me sometimes I thought I didn't want to work with staff. These can be hidden potencies you have, but don't want to be this. Be aware to this as what if anywhere you judged yourself as not being able to do or accomplish this it is actually a potency and a strength?

From my point of view, usually right before you are about to succeed at something you will hit a wall, or it will feel like there is an energy blockage. Most times when I have a new idea or new venture I start to create, I find that right before I am about do to well, I stumble and to be frank sometimes I will fall flat on my face, not literally but I usually will make what many people would judge a huge mistake. This could be I have no money coming in and everything stalls, it could be with funding that I thought I had that won't come through, a repair will need to be made that I didn't plan for, more money will need to be given out for an event I didn't budget for.... and so on... It is funny when these things happen as did we just put a ton of energy into something and now the universe is providing what we requested but it has shown up in a different way than we expected. This next time you fall flat on your face over something — I would suggest laughing. What if you don't go into judgement of yourself or of the perceived "problem". Every time I have had an "issue" that could be perceived as not fun or difficult happen within my business I have ended up making more money from it – especially if I don't go into the trauma and drama of it. It might take a bit of time but there has never been a "problem" within my business that didn't end up allowing me the opportunity to create more than I imagined. It gave me the opportunity to make a choice to do something different and to stay committed towards achieving what I knew I would like in my business. I no longer get worried when things show up chaotically.

When the unplanned event or stalled energy happens, what if it is the universe providing for you but it did not turn out exactly as you thought it would-in fact it ended up being even better? Please, the next time you have a random crazy event happen that seems like it is going to be awful and it is making it more difficult for you can you allow yourself to just laugh and know that all will be well. What if you let what shows up, show up however it needs to for you to succeed? What if whatever happens in your life or your business it is not ever a mistake but a chance to produce more abundance? Everything that happens in your business be grateful for it. I mean everything! I have found when I go into that space of gratitude towards anything that shows up it makes everything easier and more playful.

Here is something most people will not tell you, when you do thrive, not everyone will be happy for you. I bought into that if I did well in my business and had money all my "problems" would disappear. I found if I was not joyful and committed to my life this is not true about the problems disappearing as suddenly you are in a different space with a different knowing that other's may not completely get. This by far is the most difficult for me and I still have found myself stuck in at times. I am by nature not a competitive person with other people. I am competitive with myself and I always would like to continually better myself. But I don't typically compare myself with other people – and if I do I know that this is what I am doing however, I do not function here typically. I also like it when others succeed. This my friends, is not the norm. If you do well at anything in life to be frank there are people that can and will be harsh and mean towards you. This can be your friends, your co-workers, and even your family. You will feel it like it is hatred and negativity and you will want to hide and not do well as much anymore. People will stab you in the back over it, they will despise you, and make you out to be a villain. But here is the thing: absolutely none of that is true.

Once you have been in business for a while you will most likely have to find a way to out create this energy. You will have to let yourself know this energy is there though, perceive it and acknowledge it to change it but for yourself not them. When you succeed, you are making people look at their own failures straight in the face. I have struggled with this quite a bit-I don't particularly like making people feel bad. I don't consider myself a super talented person at all. I do well and I commit to succeeding but anyone could do this if they desired it. But most people simply do not want to succeed. Look at that – how many people do you know who want to succeed and have an easy, fun, life? People will say they want this-do they take the steps to make it happen? Do they make the choice to do this? Can you be honest with yourself the next time you see this weird tangled energy? If you want to create a business I am sure you will be aware of this energy – but can you only be aware of it and not the effect of it? You don't necessarily need to change the energy-you can't change people unless they would like to change but what if you don't resist it either, and know it's there instead of denying this it makes life easier.

When you are in a group of people and you feel hatred, anger or negativity can you ask yourself if this is even your feelings? Are you perceiving someone else's world and is it all messed up!? Is this jealousy? Are these people giving you a backhanded compliment when they are jealous of you? What can you do to out-create this energy? Can you not judge yourself or make it significant when this comes up? What if jealousy is when people are not creating what they truly would like in their life – and you no longer allow yourself to be paralyzed by their fears. As this is their fears-not yours. When you are working with other people or working with people at all what can you do to make yourself aware when you are in their reality and their world instead of your own? If you can get a handle on this everything will be much easier for you. Also, if you let yourself be aware when there is any of this energy from anyone else what if you acknowledge this and then let them be this energy and be whatever they need to be, with no criticism attached to it.

What if the more you have the willingness to allow everyone to be whatever they choose to be by not judging it as good or bad, it will open more space for them to maybe choose something different? This is not to say there will not be people who are supportive and helpful too. I would just allow yourself to know this may not be the case with most people and be ok with this. You are different and different is not always looked upon as greatness in this reality.

The people who do contribute and work with you with joy and ease be grateful for them and acknowledge them. The ones who don't contribute be grateful when they leave your life, and if they stay be aware of their energy and know it is not yours. Don't waste precious time and energy on people who are not supportive. When anyone judges, or reacts to you it is all about them and where they are functioning from, and has nothing to do with you. I was in one of Shannon O'Hara's classes when she brought up that if someone makes you out to be a villain it is easy with practice to transmute that energy into something else and become more productive. If someone is throwing a lot of hate at you what if you let your barriers down, receive that energy and that expand it out and turn it into something different? Can you use it as momentum to change and create what you desire? The hatred/jealousy can be turned into more energy for your business for it takes a lot of energy for someone to continually throw down such anger and jealously all the time... use their energy they are giving you to your advantage-it is a gift.

If you are doing things well your business will probably be constantly changing. Don't be afraid to make changes in your business. Don't be scared to have other sources of revenue inside your business or even outside of your business when you know that you can make money through this as well. What if money can come to you in many ways, through many different sources with very little effort? Money is only energy what would it take for you to be the magic of the energy of money? When people keep trying to maintain the status quo only, it limits them. Sometimes things will be tumultuous, disorganized and a down right mess, but you will facilitate more from it if you keep up the momentum of change and don't judge yourself, the mess and chaos. When something is disordered and destroyed this is when something new can be created. Ride the peaks and valleys of your business but stay neutral with your energy on any changes in the business. What if you don't react, resist, align or agree with any of it? Would this make the whole situation easier? However, if you do have a moment where you flip out let yourself do that and don't critic yourself for that either! What if afterwards you then allow yourself to be centered again after any freak-outs? What if you do your best to be non-judgmental of anyone who struggles with any changes you institute in your business as well? What if the people you work with you or your customers you let them be as awful as they need to be and then let them leave the business if needed or create something enchanted within the business? If you judge them you will lock in the judgement of them, when this is not true. Every single person can be anything that they would like-no one person is all good and all bad.

Another aspect I really had to get in creating a different reality in business is your identity is not your business. Your business will have its own identity on its own away from you. Recognize this-people will talk about your business like it is its own entity or person, you create a name for your business, it has a brand, it has its own customers, and it makes money. You can sell your business and someone else can run it-customers talk about your business name without identifying you as the creator in the sentence. It is not a part of you, completely. You have a family, a home, friends and activities that have nothing to do with your business as well. What if you allow yourself and your business to generate together without making it all about you, will it attribute more ease to everything? Your business will have many people who will be a part of it, and many people will contribute to it financially and want to take patronage with it. Sometimes when I am in a different space I will believe that my business can't run without me. Which is a trap, a lie, and arrogant. If someone else were to come in and take over my business it would be a change, but everything would be fine-it may be different but it would still run. What if when you are a creator you realize your creation will run on its own? What if you then ask your business what would it take for the two of you to co-create together?

In terms of your business being its own entity your business will also talk with you. It will give you advice and input. But it's an energy that will show up in a way you don't realize if you don't stay in the question and let yourself be aware of what your business is talking to you about. For example, there are many times my business will talk to me through my clients. Sometimes there will be many customers who will say they wish I had a certain product or service and I know this is my business telling me to consider it. When I do offer a new service, I will get customers who will say things about it and make more recommendations. I acknowledge this when this shows up. I don't resist it. I don't make them wrong for their recommendations. I keep asking questions on how to make things even easier and how I can make more money in the business. I also had to be willing to receive when people say nice things about my business. Sometimes this is more difficult for me then the things that could be improved upon. When you acknowledge where your business is doing well this is also your business speaking to you. What if you allow your business to talk with you and the two of you together can come up with what works for you? What if you are aware of the energy of your business you will hear and perceive the energy of it and what it requires for more success? You can ask it what can we create that we never imagined possible that would create more money than we ever imagined possible? See what shows up with this.

You will be and do all sorts of things that no one will ever tell you about with your business. This could be within your business or even with people who work with you, or business deals you are closing or negotiating. I am a bitch, a healer, a giver, a taker, an idiot, a genius, a villain, a super hero and much more. I am all of these things as a whole. I am sure that you are as well. Be aware that all of these are points of view people will have about you and they are only definitions, but none of them are real. I used to go into judgment of myself when I would be and do all of these things. Especially if I was being what most people would consider not nice. Now, I look at this and realize that I am so aware of the energy needed for my business to succeed and what the business and people within my business requires and are asking from me, that I will be whatever it takes to get the job done. What if when you cut off these parts of yourself that you perceive are negative it actually makes it more difficult for you in business? If this means people will perceive me as a bitch as they function differently in business than I do-I am ok with this. It is not even true. What if being a bitch or as I like to call a potent bitch is simply an energy only? It is not real. I am not telling you to be mean to people, what I am telling you is what if someone believes you are being mean what if that is not always necessarily true-it is just an opinion they have? I really had to look at this for myself. I have had more than a few people who worked with me tell me that I scared them. I was incredibly confused by this, then I really looked at this and realized I am honest most of the time and very direct-this makes most people scared as they do not function from this space. Do most people want honesty and directness or do they prefer to not know? How many people do you know in your life that when they judge you acting like a bitch towards them is the one thing that may create a change they have been asking for in their universe? Is this wrong or is it you caring about these people? I also started to at times soften my energy but say the same thing and it has made the communication easier too.

Can you acknowledge when you are facilitating a change for someone else out of caring? We are not victims in this world we are very responsible for what we create in our life. How many people do you know who act mean or unkind with you in business or even in life as this is the only way they know possible? But people need to make a choice then-it's up to them. I would prefer to be kind and be perceived as kind always, but that in business will not always create more for everyone. Sorry-I know that this can be the opposite of what most people will say. It's my preference to be kind, but I am aware sometimes that will NOT create more possibilities for everyone as a whole. I truly care about everyone but I cannot cut off who I am for anyone either. I used to get really upset when I could perceive others thought I was being horribly mean in business... then I had a friend point out to me if I was truly being mean would I really care if they are doing well as I do? You have to be really present and conscious though when you are the energy of being what is perceived in this world as mean or unkind. Trust and be honest with yourself. Are you trying to diminish or control someone or make them less than you, or are you aware of what more is possible for the greatness of ALL when you are the energy of being potent or what in this reality is considered mean?

By being a bitch and potent, will this energy create more for you and them, if so then be the energy that is required. If it will do nothing or make the energy or situation worse many times I will choose to withdraw my energy or ignore the person or situation completely. I am very aware and conscious when I do this with someone though and extremely present. What would it take for you to be a master of energy and know and be intensely present as to what the energy is required for your business and with everyone present within your business? Can you be all of this as well without judging yourself and be aware when people are judging you for being as powerful as you are! All of this is simply an energy-it is not wrong.

Sometimes when we do and be things as we are following the energy of what is required of each and every person or project in our business. I do let everyone do what they need to do and be on their own path to greatness. How many people do you know in your life who choose to limit themselves constantly? I again just let the energy be however it needs to be. When you create anything, you are allowing other people to step into more possibilities and to create more for themselves. They may choose it or they may not-it is simply a choice and everyone is free to do whatever is correct for them at the time.

I have made choices that are amazing and other's that I wish I had made it easier for myself, but these choices got me to where I am now which I am grateful for. I have limited myself as well too-I still do this at times but I can now more quickly get out of this space – everyone else has their own journey as well, just like you. What if we could allow everyone to be what they need to be and not go into judgement of it? What if you make the demand to have people in business and in your life who are kind, caring and fun? Ask this... see what shows up. For me it changed everything dynamically. I now find when something isn't congruent in my life or business suddenly this will change quickly to become easier. Also, the more you acknowledge yourself and your greatness and judge yourself less, the less the unkindness in people shows up. If you find that most people in your life are unkind ask what I am doing to create this in my life? Are you judging yourself? Do you allow their judgements to be more important than you? What if you simply stop that the judging yourself and everything changes?

For myself with business, I have noticed that I tend to not very often be satisfied ever. I always would like to create more than I have constantly. I used to resist this energy. I would make it bad-like why can't you be happy with what you have? Plenty of people would love to have what you have-why can't you be satisfied? When I find myself here-I go into gratitude for the greatness in my life of what I have but then I ask what would it take to have more and what else is possible that I haven't even thought of? What else is there? What more awesomeness can I add to my life? Bring it! I am ready universe! It is fine to want more in your life and more adventure you are a creator so then keep creating. Keep creating more in your life. It is ok to desire more as there is so much more that we can offer and so much more we can actualize in our life. When we desire to constantly create more in our reality to me this is being at peace with our self-what if we simply misidentified this as not being satisfied? When really if we seem unsatisfied it is only time to get to work, and create more.

Going into debt for your business is not always a bad thing. Money is everywhere. It is fun to use someone else's money when creating a business than your own. When I first started my business, I took out over 50K in debt and I made a ton of judgements on myself for that. I would think "Oh I need to pay this off quickly or I wish I had money of my own instead of taking out a loan and going into debt etc." If I had stayed in the question this would have been easier. If I had asked what will this 50k create? Will this money make my life more fun and joyful? What can I be or do to pay this debt off quickly?" If I pay attention to the energy and it feels like having this money is going to be great I don't go into doubt over going into debt anymore and I move forward with my targets. What if we look at money as what will it create more of when we play with it? If I use this 50k what more will it bring into my life? Now, when I look at this loan from 10 years ago and how quickly I paid it off and what I created with it-I don't even know why I decided to be so fearful of it. I know if I had simply stayed in the question and wasn't so negative with it I would have paid it off even faster. I probably should have taken out even more money!!!

I am not saying always go into debt, look at the situation be wise, be creative. What if debt is simply creating more and being aware of what more is possible? What if debt isn't as real as we make it seem? If you do take out money for a loan don't judge yourself. You will make more money without ANY judgements about money. What if money doesn't come from force? What if it comes from ease and relaxation?

What is it like to be in joy of business and creating beyond this reality? For me, I had to look at the energy of this. As I know I am still playing with doing this in my business now. For me this space is constantly creating with ease. This means creating everything you desire without going into judgement of how you make it happen or how it shows up.

Creating money with ease and having abundance – and not going into the "how" this shows up. It is being aware and receiving the energy of every person, place and thing and using it to your advantage. It is not going into judgement, and creating beyond whatever limitations show up. It is having no barriers, no limitations, and no resistance. It is acknowledging your potency and power of creation and to be in communion with every molecule around you. It is not judging yourself or anyone. It being in the constant state of knowing what is going on and being a master of all energies. Can you feel this space? It is the space of creation. It is a dance! Now Create!

I would like to thank Gary Douglass, Dain Heer, Shannon O'Hara, Erica Glessing, Beth Schliebe and the many other facilitators who have helped me process these ideas and creations! Much gratitude and appreciation!

What would it be like to have more play and ease in your life? I have not always functioned from this space but when I do, I notice there is more communion and fun with everything in my life. More shows up if by magic. What would it take for this to be the normal in all your relationships, with money, with business and with anything and everything you can imagine?

Anywhere you have limited yourself to not do this I would encourage you to ask for a different choice to show up. It is possible. I get it and have seen it for myself. I used to make myself wrong for many things, for creating money for myself, and for having created a great family for myself. That sounds funny that I would make myself wrong for this, right? Well, guess what-I was so aware of what everyone else thought of me I wasn't even acknowledging what was going on that worked well for me in my life. I had to acknowledge that if I make the choice to everything will come easily to me. I had to stop buying any judgment as real. As soon as I realized this and got this everything got so much more fun. What if you can do this for yourself? What if you start to acknowledge the greatness in you and what you are creating, and then not be surprised when even much more of that will show up for you-as if by magic?

Change comes at times from getting out of your comfort zone and allowing yourself to be anything and everything you choose for yourself. I invite you to explore the space of all possibilities for yourself. It is a fun and exciting place! Have done many things in my life such as worked for big companies in their marketing departments, been a high school teacher and a business consultant. By far the most fun for me has been running my wellness center for over 10 years in Peoria, AZ. I am currently known for skin care, reiki, intuitive readings, healing sessions and soul retrieval healings.

I am also an access consciousness bars and body processors practitioner. With my readings, I believe in asking generative questions to clear any blockages and ask for new possibilities and awareness to show up.

The Author

Kristen Trimmer
www.CreatingBusinessBeyondThisReality.com/kristen-trimmer

CHAPTER 13

The Business of Living – Creating Beyond

Barbara Schubert

To me creating beyond this reality is reaching out for what seems impossible right now and make it possible, becoming a living example. And whatever it is you have decided is impossible in your current situation, would you be willing to consider that this could be just a mindset you can change?

So I jump right in and I invite you now to think of and maybe even write down the things you would like to create in your life. What would you like your life to create as? Now go through that list and find out what really is your sincere wish. Make this your target. Maybe a few things can be combined and put into one. And commit to that. Make your commitment to do whatever it takes for this to actualize.

How do you know it is a sincere desire? When I make an honest commitment to myself to reach a true target whatever it takes, then I have this body sensation of a bright wave running through me, touching every cell with an intensity that could be misinterpreted as fear yet I know its deep awe and excitement about the unknown. So ask your body to tell you, to give you the clear sensation of sincere commitment for a true target. And every time you are about to choose and your body shows this sensation you know clearly... that!

When I was in a situation where I had lost everything I made the commitment to create my life anew. I did not have any idea what this was going to look like. I knew that situation I was in had to change and I was clear about the qualities I was targeting. First thing I had to do was moving into another town and so I needed to find an apartment there. I made a list of all the things that apartment had to provide for me. I like rooms filled with sunlight and a view into the sky when I look outside the window. I like shops a few minutes' walk from my home to make shopping convenient for me so all these qualities went on my list. And after I was clear about the qualities of the new home I was going to create into my life I began to mention my intentions to move into another town, looking for a place to live there, in each and every conversation I had with anyone. Within two months I had found an apartment that had exactly the qualities I had asked for and I had a handful of people together who offered me help with moving my personal things and furniture.

What for do I tell you this story? For pointing out two things that I have found very helpful and effective with creating whatever you desire in your life. For one: Your choice comes first. However crazy your choice appears to be, when your body gives you these sensations of green lights, then go for it. And be aware that you create beyond what is currently there. Maybe you are even challenging the impossible. Please dare! In my situation at that time choosing to move into another town probably was the craziest choice ever. I had no money to afford a deposit that is required for getting a flat for rent, I had no job to prove that I was able to pay the monthly rent, I had two kids with me and I was totally and alone responsible for them, I had no car to move my stuff and again no money to pay a moving service. I just had the knowing that I had to move. And I had the willingness to ask for help and receive it. And so I found out that an old school friend of mine I had not seen for at least twenty years worked in the office of a housekeeping company. An apartment was getting free and she immediately reserved it for me. She arranged that I did not have to pay the deposit straight away and also that regarding rent I could pay as much as I could afford and they gave me a year time to make my account even. Parents of schoolmates of my kids walked up to me offering to move my things from one town to the other with their cars. Whatever it is you are about to create, make your choice, ask for contribution and be prepared to receive miracles.

And second: Your body provides and perceives the information for creating with ease. When you desire a new pen to write, what do you ask for? Do you ask maybe for a green pen with golden glitter that writes smoothly and fits exactly into your hand giving you a great pleasure when writing with it? Guess what happens when a blue pen with silver glitter is directly in front of your nose that has all the qualities you desire for a good writing experience? Yes, most likely you will not recognize it as such, because it is not green with golden glitter. When asking for my new home I had no imagination about what it was supposed to look like. I listened to what my body required to thrive there. I had no image. I went for the quality and followed this energy my body told me... that!

Do you say now, but it is important for me that it looks exactly so? Yes, acknowledge that importance, yes, this is important for you... Do you notice a change when you repeat that this specific look is important for you? Do you still defend it as that significant? Perhaps you smile now... then you know it's not as important as you thought it is. Now you have created more space for you to choose what is really yours. With your mind you can visualize and create images. Following the wisdom of your body allows you to create with much more elegance. And I invite you to the joy of creating with ease.

One day I walked on the street. My separated husband had threatened me that he would ruin me. Typical divorce fight, as I know

now. At that time it struck me without warning, I was not prepared for meanness and I was deeply upset. I did not have the money to afford an advocate. So while I was walking down the road I kept repeating a question in my mind: Who can help me here? I was not paying any attention to the people around me. A voice reached me through my thoughts calling: Hey! Hello! Wait! And I raised my head and out of the crowd I saw a tall man quickly walking over to me. As he stood before me, he looked into my eyes with such gentleness and spoke the words: Everything will be alright. All is in God's hand. And he handed me a book that said: The beauty of the self. I looked at him confused about that situation and told him, that I did not have money with me to purchase a book. That actually was the truth, my purse was empty. He smiled: I don't sell the book, you give what you can. Take it, please! And went back to his place at the side of the road. Somehow his words had comforted me. And as I slowly walked on I concluded when all is in gods hand and everything will be alright then everything includes me and I will be alright.

A strange thought for me not following any religious practice, yet it set me at ease in that moment. I realized that my feet had stopped walking and I looked up and saw that I was standing at the front door of my bank. So following an impulse and without thinking I went inside and took some money from the little money I had on my account, folded it as I usually do and returned to that man. I gave it to him: Here, I have folded in kindness, respect and gratitude. He looked at me and slowly repeated my words. And he kept looking at me in silence and then he said: I did not expect you to come back. Thank you.

That man with his simplicity got me out of my troubled state of mind. He saw my worries through the crowd and he came to comfort me with what he was able to offer me. An act of total vulnerability and caring. And it was my willingness to receive his kindness in that moment that changed my day.

What do we normally do when a stranger walks up to us and especially when it's a certain type of stranger like a homeless, a beggar or as in this case a member of a spiritual sectarian group? We put our barriers up high and communication becomes jerky, if not impossible. Lowering the barriers opens up new possibilities and expands the awareness so that you can receive what is there in every moment.

You know, and very soon after that encounter an old friend showed up I had not met for many years and he gifted me with some money. And so I could afford the advocate.

Ask and you shall receive, we read in a book of wisdom. The universe is always and persistently working on your behalf. Be willing to receive the unexpected blessings on the way and be ready to gift, following your inner knowing.

Creating beyond this reality to me is also creating beyond what I think this reality is. What do you say when someone sticks their nose into your things? Right. That's none of your business so what is my business, I wonder? Is this reality my business? Is what I believe this reality is my business?

May I ask you a weird question: Are you happy with your life? If not as a whole, are you happy with some parts of your life? When you find something in your life that you are happy with, would you be willing to acknowledge that there you have created beyond this reality? Look around you. This reality is not about being happy, it is not about enjoying what you have, it's not about having fun with what you do. This world is about struggling for what you do not have, defending what you got and rejecting what you do not like. So when you have managed to create happiness somewhere in your life you have created outside the box. You have made choices to create and maintain your happiness beyond an average of unhappiness. I invite you to look at these areas in your life and perceive the energy of that, become aware of the energetic quality of the choices you made to create your happiness. That! Follow this energy. When you perceive it anywhere, go for it. The more you become aware of that energy of happy choices and actually choose them, the more you train the muscle of creating beyond this reality.

One day I went to the shop, selected a really expensive fine textile and ordered a curtain for my kitchen window. It was such a pleasure to do that. And it was not only that I could afford it, it was not just about the money. It was the feeling that I had created this. I had taken the steps to get there. That feeling of I can do it, I can make it.

So would you take a moment here and look at your life, at what you have achieved and what more would you like to create? Would you be willing to acknowledge your achievements and your willingness to take it even further?

This feeling proud of me and the gratitude for everyone and everything that contributed to me on the way I find are most valuable boosters for creating beyond.

Find that feeling within you, find a situation where you had this pride and joy of achieving and abundance. Take that feeling and nurture it, this knowing about your capacities and capability to reach your targets. Make it an anchor. Maybe you even find a little thing that reminds you of your potency when you begin to doubt yourself. And go ahead, keep creating.

After separating a severe illness forced me to quit job and close my practice for body energetics and facilitating I was totally exhausted, my body skinny to the bones, no money, no income, nothing to sell, all friends gone, family turned away except my mother. I had lost nearly everything and almost my body, too. People were getting hard on me how I could leave that man. In fact, they were leaning back watching me and there were bets about how long it was going to take until I utterly fail and have to go back to him in order to survive with the two children. Not exactly a situation anyone would like to stick with for long. I was very aware that I had created my situation with the choices that I had made in the past putting everyone's needs above me and totally leaving myself out of the equation. So I was willing to choose different and take the steps required to change this.

And in this situation of having nothing I choose the impossible. I signed in for a three year training, not knowing how to afford the costs or who would look after my children while I was attending class. I just knew I had to do it. And I asked, where can I get help? Who is willing and able to help? I did not only ask, I was the question personified. Every cell of me was ready to receive any help that could possibly contribute to me.

And the second choice that I made was taking a deep breath and applying for social welfare. That was an act of total exposure, I felt like naked. And while I told that lady my situation I saw the shock in her response and she immediately filled out all the forms so that I got the financial aid right away. I was totally grateful that I lived in a country that offered such help and for the kindness of that lady to quicken up the procedure for me And in that moment of gratitude I realized that I had bought into the medical point of view that after such an illness as I had the body must be too weak to work and recovery takes a long time. So I made the commitment that I would do whatever it takes to change this. I found a practitioner who gifted me with body sessions for a minor charge, I found a job and I started giving sessions again. And money showed up as if by magic and was always there when I had to make my payments and it was always more than I had to spend.

It is the willingness to be humble and ask for help, the gratitude of receiving and the commitment to do whatever is required that allows more possibilities to pop up and create change. So I invite you to ask yourself some questions when you are in a situation you would like to change. What choice created this? Who can I ask for contribution? What am I willing to receive? What is required here? And taking this further, what about not waiting for a lack to be ready to receive, what about asking for money and possibilities to show up when things are going fine for you? Does that sound like fun?

When others are convinced they know what is best for you, what you should create your life as and whom you are supposed to live with, is there anything you have to do about that? I built a muscle for stating to such people with a smile, silent in my mind first and then even aloud: That's none of your business. And I confirm to myself, that what they say and think about me truly is not my business. In my twenties one of my teachers used to say, that what people say about you always is a statement about themselves. And the thing is, for whatever reason, we seem to forget what we know from time to time. And the point is not to judge ourselves when we realize that we have chosen against our knowing, the point is to celebrate that awareness and choose different, choose what we know, no matter how crazy it seems.

Have you found that loosing, separating and other obstacles encourage you to collect all your power and increase your drive to create? Not at all, a little or a lot? Would you be willing to acknowledge your capacity to turn anything that occurs into a contribution for you?

What have we learned in this reality? We can only do one thing or the other. We cannot have it all. Either we create with people which equals we have to compromise, or we are not willing to compromise for long on what is true for us. Or we have to do it completely on our own which means we have to exclude everyone eventually. Does this work for you: either an unlucky compromise or having everything under your control? Maybe you are a little control freak? Would you be willing to consider another possibility? What about choosing what contributes to you in the first place? What about choosing that adds to your way with ease? And what about the possibility of you being totally in charge while allowing contribution to make things easier and more joyful for you? How much more could you create?

Maybe by now you begin to think that these examples seem quite down to the basics of living in this reality, so where is the creating beyond this reality? And where is the ease? Yes, I totally get you. Ease is not necessarily the easy way and not always found in the way that provides everything to the princess without even mentioning a wish, preferably delivered by the magic prince charming Ease and joy is found in the flow that comes when receiving everything without a fixed point of view and choosing without being focused on a certain outcome. As the mantra of Access Consciousness® puts it so beautifully: All of life comes to me with ease and joy and glory®. All of life means you have to be willing to receive everything, the good, the bad, the ugly and all the rest, make your choices and keep going, no matter what happens.

There is this opinion that creating beyond equals riches and an upper class lifestyle and there is this believe that creating beyond is easy for those who already are somehow great. Take a close look at these opinions. Can you see that this is a mindset totally inside the box? It is this reality that announces only the rich and famous go beyond.

And I would like to point out that creating beyond is possible from right where you currently are. It is not a privilege of wealthy people, not a privilege of educated people, not a privilege of a social or financial status, color, sex, culture, family, religion or political structure. I share ways and tools with you that you can apply in any situation you are right now and for any issue you may have. These tools have worked and still do work for me and they can work for you, if you choose them. Now having said that, I add what I always said to my children and I also say it to my customers: never simply believe what anyone says, even when it makes a lot of sense to you. Take it as an information, do not make it a recipe. Go and check for yourself. Find out what's true for you and do that. You know.

There is also this mindset that putting money aside and never touching it, never using it is a privilege of the very rich ones in this world. If this is part of your mindset I invite you to change it now. I tell you how I started creating wealth from literally nothing. I always have put and I still do put 20 percent of my income aside and I set targets without an expectation of when or how to reach it. One of my targets for example was to have aside the amount that equals one year for the rent I had to pay for my apartment at that time. When I set this target I did not even have an income. I just knew I will have that amount of money someday, however I was going to get the money together. And of course I did. And once I had that amount I let it work for me creating even more for me. When you make a choice and you are willing to do what is required to get there and not limit yourself with a certain way or a fixed date when to reach it you have all chances to have what you target.

10 per cent of my income are for my ease, my thank you for me for creating. And this money I never spend. Yes. You can start right now. Take 100 in your currency. Now 10 percent is 10, right. So every time you get 100 you put aside 10 for you and so your wealth grows continuously. So you nurture your self-esteem with creating more and your gratitude grows.

And the other 10 percent I put aside for joy. Yes. I enjoy travelling. So with every ten percent I put aside I am nurturing my pleasure of travelling. What joy can you nurture?

And please be aware that this is not about saving money. This is about celebrating you, your capacity to create and nurturing your gratitude for you and joy about you. I have found that joy and gratitude are magnificent creators that take you with ease wherever you are heading and beyond.

Are you now willing to have that?

One time in a discussion I explained my view of things and what possibilities I believe are available. The interesting response was the suggestion I should go to a psychotherapist because my problem obviously was so deep that I needed a specialist to overcome it. Did I go to a therapist? Certainly not. I follow my inner knowing.

So whoever it is that diagnoses something is wrong with you and that you need therapy, do not quickly buy into that, do not let that stop you and get you into doubting you. Please consider that what you are able to perceive may be beyond their horizons. Always follow what you know and listen to people that do not judge you. Be aware that most of the time what people tell you about you is just about themselves.

So take a situation in your life where someone told you things about you that made you just sit there kind of paralyzed, not really knowing what to think of that, made you feel small and of no value. Now turn that around as if the person was not talking about you, as if that person was talking about themselves. Do the words make more sense now? Mostly they do. So this is not your business then. Simply thank them for their suggestion and keep going on your path.

Your thoughts create. So I invite you to stop repeating crap. Seriously. Please observe. Look at what you repeat continuously in your words and thoughts. Become aware of these little quotes and automatic responses. Sometimes we even find them funny. That's ok. Just do not believe that stuff. If you choose to keep saying these words then say them consciously with a laugh inside hhh, I say this hhh, how funny that I say this.

When I was in this period of separating and divorcing I kept repeating: this fighting for divorce makes me so tired and sick. My mindset was: separation equals fighting for what is true for me and that affects my health and exhausts me. Is it not interesting that I created exactly that? Once I realized that and shifted my mindset divorce took place with ease. What I did not realize at that time that I had another mindset running in the background that said separating equals leaving everything behind and starting anew from nothing. Isn't it funny? Your thoughts create. So if you are a control freak who desires to control everything, here is your realm: control your thoughts, control these automatisms and shift them to serve you with creating beyond.

We think we need a plan, have to know a recipe, follow step after step some instructions, and be on the right path to reach our targets. I have found that exactly that planning and expecting things to occur according to a plan limits and restricts the actualization of what I am creating. Chaos is an infinite creative source and a great creator. Creating beyond is creating outside the box. Determining plans and steps precisely in advance you can only do from the past, from experience, from the comfort of the proved. What if that was your box and from there you can create your future only as a repetition of what you are used to? It's not always the big choices, it's the simple choices every day that make the difference. To create beyond you have to choose different, you have to walk an unknown path.

So what do you know? What does your inner voice tell you to create that your mind considers as total impossibility?

Creating beyond this reality also is creating what others think that is impossible in your current situation. Would you consider that when you have an idea to create it could also be possible for you to actualize it? Or why else would you have that idea if not because you are the one to create it?

Every time I make the choice to create my life totally beyond everything I have created before I follow my inner knowing and ways show up as if by magic. Your life is your business. Know that you know. Please follow your knowing, whatever that is and wherever outside the box it leads you, keep going. The earth calls for courageous people like you who dare to create beyond. Thank you.

What is success? When am I successful?

What distracts you? And I am grateful for the clarity the slogan of access consciousness is Empowering people to know that they know. And that's exactly what it does and is. And I am grateful for this. And gratitude is one of the most powerful creators. When I was facing those challenging times I was grateful for every little thing, for the food on the table, for the shelter of my simple home, for my two wonderful children, for the smile of a stranger passing by, for my body serving me so well, for all the help kind people gifted me with...

Some say when you have been down to the ground you lose the fear of losing. This is true for me...

The Author

Barbara Schubert

www.CreatingBusinessBeyondThisReality.com/barbara-schubert

CHAPTER 14

A Badass Business

BENOIT TRUDEL

A business requires sound and solid building blocks to succeed, most would say. And many would agree that you need a good business plan, enough capital, an entrepreneur to manage the business, marketing skills, time, willingness to take risks, and many other factors that we believe that when combined, will result in a strong business.

When I was a teenager, I was well aware of how others see working in a typical 9 to 5 job. It is something that you dread to start on Monday and escape from on Friday. You are confined to a role and you execute the tasks assigned to you by your boss, with limited maneuvering room for creativity. The gains of your work contribute mainly to someone else, a company removed from you. Starting your own business then appears as a way to have your own freedom, be your own boss, have more flexibility, set your own hours, create for you and be in the driver's seat! And how well does that work out for many entrepreneurs?

I have always been a creator, an entrepreneur at heart, making and building things since I was little. At the age of 16, I got a job cleaning rooms in a new apartment building complex where they had offered new tenants one year of free maid service. Once the year was over, the administration of the building did not wish to continue to offer the service, so I took on the clients as a free-lancer and soon recognized the opportunity and registered my first business as Masterclean Ltd, a maid service which I managed for 3 years. I build up a good clientele, had 4 employees at one time and the business grew to a certain point. However, the building blocks I used for my business were based on many points of view which I had picked up from others: you need a sound business plan and to work hard, it takes 3 years for a business to be profitable, charge less and have more clients, work on weekends, no one can do it better than you so you must do it all, keep your clients happy, and many more points of view.

After 3 years, I was truly exhausted. I was not making any money, barely surviving, I could not do more than I was already doing working 7 days per week, and I was constantly worried about keeping my clients happy, being successful and doing it right. There was little joy or creativity left. When I decided to close the business, there was a sense that I was leaving things unfinished and that I knew more was possible but that I did not know how to make it work. And now, 30 years later, I am ready to start over in a completely different way.

The tools of Access Consciousness® are like building blocks for me, where I can play and discover what I desire to create. What if there is a totally different way to create a business that can work for you, be fun for you, and make it possible for the business to grow and thrive into the profitable creation that you know is possible? Does having a business need to be hard? Is there another way? Are you willing to be successful whatever that looks like? What if your thoughts do create your reality, and it was simply a matter of changing how you see businesses in order to create what you know is possible?

Let's explore the notion of *"your thoughts create your reality"* and see what we can discover. What if all judgments and perceptions were lies and fabrication, and it was just a matter of being aware of them, not fixing, understanding or changing them, but rather choosing to let them go and create a different reality? Sounds too easy? Let's give it a go.

I invite you to take a few sheets of paper and write at the top – *I can't have a thriving successful business because*... And then write underneath as many reasons that you can come up with which you believe to be true. For myself, I would put – because I don't have enough money, I am alone and don't know where to start, I am a single dad with 2 kids to take care of and need financial stability, there is so much competition out there, what if I fail, etc. Do not censure yourself and write down especially the crazy ones. All of these are the points of view that limit and prevent you from creating a thriving business. Now go over each one and then use the Access Consciousness tool – **Interesting point of view, I have that point of view**. For example – *I can't have a thriving business because I don't have enough money – Interesting point of view, I have that point of view*. Repeat it to yourself a few times for each belief that you wrote down. This may take a while and you may feel a bit silly, and what if that is all it takes to change your reality? What happens with this tool is that it releases the charge that you have which then allows for more space for possibilities and for the limitations to dissolve.

I have always believed the notion that if you can see it and imagine it, you can create it. And in Access Consciousness, a great and fun tool is the **energy ball**. Imagine your business, as a ball in front of you and like a melting pot, pull in the different ingredients that would make it fun for you. For me, I invite co-creation with others with different flavors of fun, outrageousness, vulnerability, creation and innovation. I invite wealth, beauty, money, comfort, luxury, nature in the mix. I see myself connecting and facilitating thousands of people, creating a space for change, allowance, exploration and joy. I allow a team to support and contribute to my business with their unique gifts and capacities, expanding it into all that it can be. I travel the globe and connect with each and every corner of the planet and its people, discovering, sharing and being more. What do YOU choose to add to create your business?

Now pull in energies from the entire universe into the ball, lighting it up and increasing its intensity, flowing into you and through every molecule of your body, then out through your head, your arms back into the world. And back to the ball, through you, out to the world and this time, tell everyone and everything that can be a contribution, that you are willing and ready to receive them now or when the time is right. Imagine a trickle of energy coming from them to the energy ball and contributing to make it brighter. Will you commit to do this exercise every day? The energy of what your business can be will then attract the things and people that it requires to grow.

I have functioned from conclusions for a long time, thinking that being right rules the world of business and my life. I never imagined that this creates limitations nor dreamed that asking questions is a much more powerful way to create. Being right is all about decisions, judgment, conclusions, computations, expectations and projections: If I offer this service or do this promotion, many people will sign up and I will make so much money. The more I work and get done, the more successful my business will be. What if all of that was not necessarily true? What if instead, I could follow the joy of what feels light for me to be and do with my business? That tool is called **light and heavy**: What feels light is true, what feels heavy is a lie. And it goes hand in hand with asking questions. *Hey business, what would you like to create today*? And see what awareness comes up. You may think of making an ad, calling someone or even something unrelated like going for a walk. Do not look for an answer, simply follow what is light. *Business, how much would be fun for you to charge for this online call*? And get a sense of the amount that comes up for you. *Business, would you like to schedule a class this month or next month*? Which one feels light to YOU? The more you do this, the more you learn to trust yourself and your awareness to guide you beyond the limited conclusions of what is right. This also fundamentally changes the dynamic from pushing, forcing and doing to a more gentle approach of listening, wondering and playing.

We have many points of view about charging for services, assuming that if we charge less, more people will be able to afford it and we will sell more products or services. And what if that is not true? I have also kept my service fees very low for some time, providing a discounted price. What if this low price is not congruent with who I am and what I would like to receive? What if a higher price would actually be the invitation for people to receive what I am willing to offer, and what they can receive? Are you willing to play with light and heavy, questions and wonder with your business? I have since raised my prices simply because it is light for me, and I am now choosing to receive more. I have had the point of view for a long time that I want to give, and that receiving money in exchange is wrong or bad. I should charge the least amount possible and give as much as I can. I have since realized that this vow of poverty is very limiting and it will not allow me and my business to grow to the extent that I would like to. I am now also willing to give, AND to learn how to receive more.

Another tool is to acknowledge what you have accomplished, what you have started to create, even if it is not yet actualized or where you would like it to be. **Acknowledgment** and **gratitude** is like planting a seed in the ground and putting water every day, taking care of it. If you stop, the plant dies. If you take care of it, be grateful for what you have created, the contacts with people you made, the money you received, the one client who came today, that will do more to grow your business than to criticize yourself for not doing enough. Would you be willing to be gentle and kind to yourself and your business, and even talk to your business like you would to a friend? What if that created the space for ease, magic and joy as well as the invitation for your business to grow, just like you would encourage a young child who stumbles and falls?

Choice creates awareness and not the other way around. And if you avoid and wait for the awareness to come, you may actually not take action. Make a choice for what feels light, and you can choose again in 10 seconds when you get an awareness of whether it works for you or not. And then you can choose again. What if growing your business is about taking one step and choosing, then asking questions and tuning into your awareness to get a sense of what works and how you can take it forward? What if it could really be that easy and fun?

I have been living and working in Tbilisi, Georgia, where I am the first Bars Facilitator. When I launched my Access business, eager to get clients for sessions and for my classes, I decided that step one would be to hold an information session and invite people to learn about this approach, sure that they would sign up for a session or a class. I did all the right things with a carefully thought out plan, a brochure, the advertisement and the word of mouth. I even did a demonstration of a Bars session and everyone loved it. And yet, this did not result in any clients. I was so disappointed. And then I held another information session a couple of months later which was a resounding success from the feedback of the attendees. Still, no one signed up. At first I made myself wrong and I then started to look at the many points of view which I have about businesses, the main one being that growth is linear and $1 + 1 = 2$. I have since demanded of myself to create a thriving business, no matter what it looks like.

I have started to have fun and to grow my business in unexpected ways. I contacted radio stations in Georgia and Armenia and offered to be a guest on their show. In a 2 week span, both radio stations called me in to talk about my life and Access Consciousness. I knew that if I tried to plan and practice what I wanted to say, in the past this had led me to be more anxious to say the right thing. So I told myself to be in question, ask what the show was ready to hear and jumped in with 2 feet. I had so much fun that they extended the first radio show from 1 hour by an extra 30 minutes. How does it get any better than this?

I also facilitated a money class with 4 online calls. For the first two, I was well prepared and nervous. I wanted to do it right. For the last

2, I went into question, followed the energy and invited the contribution from everyone and that allowed for the unknown to shape
the call. Both were so much fun, and I was so grateful for the opportunity to explore and expand how I am with my business. There was
the freedom, the creativity and the fun that I had been looking for
and I knew was possible.

By now you may have some idea about what is a **badass business**.
It is one with few rules if any, creative and fun, ad hoc and adaptive
with little or no consideration for what the business should be and
look like. I now get more and more how growing a business is not
linear nor is it about having a solid plan, or about getting it right.
It is truly like writing a book as you go, knowing that there are no
rules and that at any moment, you can create and follow the energy
of what is fun and light, asking questions, choosing, taking a step
and looking at what that has created, not from the space of judgment, but to acknowledge and tune into how it can be even more
and greater. I still bring the business, finance and marketing skills
that I have to contribution, AND there is so much more. What do
you know about growing a business that is true for you that no one
else knows, and that can be fun and an inspiration, a contribution
to your community and the Earth? What if creating your unique
business could be an invitation for others to follow? Give it a go and
show us what YOU know.

The Author

Benoit Trudel

www.CreatingBusinessBeyondThisReality.com/benoit-trudel

CHAPTER 15

Building a Business with JOY

BETH SEGALOFF

Ever since I was a young girl, my dreams of the future included helping other people and being a mom. They didn't include running a business. However, my story and life experiences over the years took unexpected paths that ultimately led to the establishment of the Tree of Life Center, which provides individual and group therapy, workshops, Reiki healing, yoga, and Access Consciousness tools. As I reflect back, I see with clarity how the foundation was set and the path to my business was created in **joy, love, faith, and self-discovery.**

By age 30 I earned a master's degree in social work, was married, and had an infant son and a fulfilling job as a school social worker, working with children with learning disabilities and emotional needs. My "plans" and expectations were simple: a loving family and a career of inspiration and service. However, my marriage dissolved when my son was two and I entered a new and challenging phase of life. I knew our divorce was "right" for me but living in suburbia as a single working mom I never felt like I fit in. I often felt alone, stressed, scared and overwhelmed. At the same time, I regained confidence and the power of choice. I was devoted to creating a home filled with love and ease.

For fifteen years, I worked in several schools and was inspired to make a difference in an educational setting. I adored the kids, but on the playground, at lunch tables, and in classrooms, I saw bullying, isolation, fear and worry. I witnessed how this affected their learning, their ability to be open in the classroom, and especially their beliefs about themselves and others. Feelings of not being worthy, pretty or smart enough settle into the mind and body at a young age, hiding the truth that all children are perfect exactly as they are. Through talk and play therapy, I formed powerful connections with the children, their families and my colleagues, but always sensed there was more I wanted to do on a professional level.

I was fortunate to find love again with my true soul mate. Ben and I fell in love in an instant. He was an Army Captain, a true humanitarian, working in international disaster relief and, as his friend once said, "a warrior for peace." He was a hero to many, including me and my son. He treated and loved Danny as his own; they had a particularly beautiful relationship. Ben brought out the best parts of me and awakened my zest for life. I felt safe, seen, loved, and inspired to experience, explore, learn and share. We were a team, a partnership, with a shared vision of a future that included family, faith and serving others together.

Then the unimaginable happened. When Ben was deployed to Afghanistan, I knew that our relationship would have to withstand uncertainty and added demands. A wedding and reception on the beach were planned for a month after his return. Nothing prepared me for October 2, 2009, when two men in uniform showed up at my door and told me Ben had been killed by a suicide bomb. I was thrust into total darkness. The shock, pain and despair were incomprehensible. The life I envisioned was taken violently and I was shattered. I now had first-hand knowledge that life is short and can change course in an instant.

After Ben's death, I questioned my place and my purpose on this earth. How was I going to raise my son with the knowledge that life can feel so unfair? How could I trust a world that allowed random violence to destroy such an extraordinary man? Who was I now and where did I fit in? Divorced and widowed by the age of 35 was not the "happily ever after" life I expected.

While in this space, I somehow managed to get my ass up and moving every day. I kept up with all the mom responsibilities and spent more time snuggling, reading, playing games and loving my son. I knew deep down that love was really all that mattered.

I realized the best way to continue Ben's legacy was to live my own life fully. I wanted to honor him by being the woman he fell in love with and more. I wanted my life to be filled with the love, goodness and inspiration he had shown me. This meant accepting exactly where I was in the "new normal", practicing ways to be in the preset moment as well as setting intentions for visions of my future. Solace and hope would arise and they were real, but a second later grief, anger, and loneliness would knock me down again. My life felt like a rollercoaster.

My healing and growth required more than talk therapy, although talking and processing were and continue to be crucial pieces. I connected with others who understood and could sit with me in the grief, especially the American Widow Project. The founder's husband was killed in Iraq and she knew the importance of connecting with other women who shared similar circumstances. The organization has retreats where women come together for healing and hope. I participated in a few and they were the perfect place for me during that time.

One weekend in Austin, Texas, I and 12 other women were led through a series of challenges, such as walking on glass and breaking an arrow with our throats (yes, I did that). These elements were presented as metaphors to overcome fear and face the limiting beliefs that were holding us back. When I allowed discomfort in and was mindful of it, I experienced profound release! Getting out of my comfort zone, facing my fears, and forming true loving connections with women who shared my pain created a powerful shift in me. I found peace and awareness sitting in mediation, which I was ready to integrate into my day to day life.

I started practicing yoga in my mid-twenties, mostly for stretching and a "sprinkle on the top" of competitive running and other exercise routines. A few years after Ben's passing, there was a dramatic shift in my yoga practice. My body and mind were in desperate need of rest as I had been in fight/flight and survival mode for so long. The benefits of yoga unfolded as I witnessed my body, breath and mind letting go and surrendering.

I realized I could choose to either wallow in loneliness or do something positive. Believe me, I have done both and I accept when there are times that I need to allow the sadness in and stay on the couch for a while. However, I also had a desire to live fully! Choosing to say YES to new experiences makes me feel alive, authentic, whole and connected.

So I dipped my toes into other holistic and "non-traditional" approaches that often seemed weird or silly to others. I took a service/surfing trip to Panama, learned to walk on hot coals, trained for and ran a marathon, discovered my creativity as a writer, and began assisting with programs at the Kripalu Yoga and Wellness Center. I was already naturally stepping into leadership roles. After I received Reiki from a friend, I was seeped in calmness, connection to spirit and a sense of "coming home" to myself. Each new encounter shed more light and created more hope. I began to experience moments of solace, peace, comfort, fun and JOY. I even adopted a personal mantra: "SPARKLE JOY".

I was falling in love with my authentic self, not just the woman Ben loved, and becoming my own hero. I started to walk, skip and run down the path of self-discovery, which continues to lead me to amazing places! I noticed both the dark and the light, joy and pain, challenges and celebrations. Grief was just one piece of the puzzle. The thirty years of my life before Ben still required nourishing, but now my heart was open and I had the tools and awareness to work through those older wounds.

There was never one 'Aha' moment when I decided to start my own business but by aligning with my truth, I was making choices from a space of love, faith and clarity. I knew I desired a change from my current job and I also wanted to share my experiences of healing and joy with others as a way to support their needs.

I began to take steps to gain skills that mirrored my own self-discovery, becoming certified in those areas that had helped me heal and that could also serve others. Within a few years I was trained as a Reiki Master, Yoga Teacher and Access Bars facilitator, and became a Certified Fire-Walking Instructor.

While still working part-time as a school social worker, I rented my own office space and hung out my shingle. But then doubts arose. Was I really going to leave the structure of a job and security of a paycheck for a complete unknown? I was a social worker, not an entrepreneur. I knew little about marketing, technology or finance. When people asked me what I wanted to do, my response was "to help people", which was clear to me but not to them. I struggled with feeling judgement from others and myself, fear of failure, and a sense of "what the heck are you doing?"

Then I said to myself, "Change the story, ask the right questions, align yourself with people you respect, collaborate and learn together, be open and awake and do what feels light in your heart". As Tosha Silver, author of "Outrageous Openness, Letting the Divine Take the Lead" writes, "Hold the question in your heart. Ask with complete focus and conviction for the Universe's guidance. Then let go and see what bread crumbs come for you to follow. If you don't get an answer, just keep asking for a while until you do."

My determination and ability to notice the bread crumbs was what guided me. Moments of awareness and awakening created space to see and explore my options. As those moments multiplied and more opportunities arose, I trusted my intuition and said YES with conviction. From this conscious awareness, I took the leap of faith, left my job and created the Tree of Life Center – a venue that acts as a lighthouse and provides space for holistic integration and transformation of mind, body and spirit.

Tree of Life offers various modalities for diverse populations and needs. There is individual coaching and counseling in person and virtually, Reiki energy healing, Yoga and Access Bars. I emphasize that emotions and beliefs are tied to life stories, which can entangle and keep us feeling "stuck", depending on how they are perceived. I ask, what if you had the power to make choices to write your story the way you desire. What if you could let go and walk through fear and worry with self-love? What if you were willing to truly look in the mirror and see all of you? What else would be possible?

I facilitate groups for people struggling with similar life experiences, such as divorce, loss, infertility, parenting, or living with illness. Some need to make specific changes in their lives, such as career changes, while others want to reduce stress or uncertainty. Regardless of the issue, there is something profound and transformative about being with others who "get it". During our time together we learn strategies, tools and coping skills, identify and foster resiliency, practice mindfulness, and learn to live in the moment and envision and attain dreams and goals.

I also lead Corporate Wellness Programs designed to create a more productive and healthy work environment that increases the business's bottom line and sustains an environment where people love coming to work! Sessions includes discussion and hands-on experiences to increase mindfulness, cohesiveness and motivation, improve communication skills, and learn coping strategies to manage stress and create balance. Workshops build and enhance a positive work culture.

All individual and group sessions and workshops are designed to integrate body, mind and spirit. Modalities used depend on where each client or group is and may include everything from meditation and yoga, to breaking boards with bare hands, walking on broken glass, or participation in a fire-walk!

Tree of Life's experiential approach creates trusting relationships and space for people to quiet the mind, observe and notice. This can be messy and uncomfortable but ultimately freeing. It does not mean that difficult experiences and emotions are erased. It is not about "moving on," but rather acknowledging the messy and "moving through" it differently.

I guide my clients and voice my point of view that there is NO fixing! You are perfect exactly as you are in this moment. Whether we are in my office talking one-on-one, connected virtually, practicing tree pose or walking across broken glass together, the "answers" are already within you. Everything that has happened in your life is part of your story and offers an opportunity to live from a conscious open heart. We can always choose how to write the next word, page, or chapter of our lives.

When people are ready to explore life changes, I ask them to consider where they feel "stuck" or stressed. Perhaps it's a relationship or a challenging work situation. Then we explore what emotions are connected to this "stuck" feeling – despair, hopelessness, and judgment, lack of self-worth or confidence? We often make choices from places of stress and negativity. What if you could re-train your brain by relaxing and restoring your physical body, calming your mind, softening your heart, and becoming your most unconditional and loving best friend? When you make choices from this space, dreams manifest themselves.

Building a business is joyful, scary, enlightening, healing, and inspiring. I created mine from past wounds and healing experiences, and I continue to accept and embrace the peaks and valleys both personally and professionally. I must continuously balance my passion, creativity and commitment with time for reflection, prayer and restoration.

I find immense JOY in sharing and serving others. I am grateful to be able to facilitate skills and strategies to guide clients and students in a sacred trusting space so that they discover their authentic selves.

My offerings continue to expand! I keep asking myself, what else is possible? By listening to my intuition and creating from a space of pure authenticity and intent to serve, it's happening and its magic!

The Author

Beth Segaloff

www.CreatingBusinessBeyondThisReality.com/beth-segaloff

CHAPTER 16

The Entrepreneurial Mindset

WENDY DILLARD

The Big Launch

I was filled with anticipation & excitement. After all, I felt like I'd been waiting for ages to finally get this new venture rolling. And in this one moment, there I was ready to take the long-awaited plunge toward my new dream business. It all seemed to come down to this one surreal moment in time. I was ready. I was ready to click the button to run my Facebook ad which would launch my new offering!

In preparation for this, I'd been actively engaged in internet marketing training for 18 months – to learn how to use online marketing tools & strategies. Along the way, I'd overcome so many personal struggles that tried to sabotage my moving forward. I overcame the many technology challenges as I learned new software. My free e-book was written... and I'd even created an audio version (for those too busy to actually find the time to read). My auto-responder email series was ready. My online sales page was ready (including a video of me explaining my offering). My new merchant account was ready to take payments. I felt such a powerful sense of accomplishment.

As an aside: I totally understand why so many want-to-be entrepreneurs only dream of owning & running an *online business*... because as much potential freedom as there can be with a successful online business, it requires tons of dedication, focus, and action. Thank goodness I love the journey as much as the destination!

So back to the story: There I was; I'd done the work and now I was ready to reap the rewards. What a high!

My Facebook ad was *the* step where I announced to the world that I was open for business. I had pinned a lot of hopes, dreams & expectations on this one little Facebook ad because its job was to attract my new paying customers. I had it all planned out. My prospects would view my online opt-in page that told them all about the benefits of my free e-book in exchange for their email address. And then, my auto-responder emails & online sales page would do the rest. So, each day, I checked my stats to see how well my ad was performing. My stats were indicating a good number of people showing interest because they *were* clicking on my ad; and I was really pleased in that respect. But, I didn't actually have many people opting-in to receive my free e-book. Although my opt-in rate was lower than I had hoped, I wasn't totally surprised because I had purposely provided very specific information on my opt-in page. By doing this, I was *only* targeting people that would seriously fit the service I was offering. I'd learned that an opt-in page could *either* bring in a bunch of curiosity seekers (by providing very general information) or I could get highly targeted leads (by providing very specific information where the viewer had a really good sense of what they would be getting from my e-book & me). And I opted for the highly targeted leads approach.

After 3 weeks of my ad running with so few opt-ins, I felt it was time to pull the plug on the ad to re-evaluate. I knew I needed to take a step back to see if I could figure out what I could do differently. It was time to re-examine each piece of my launch sequence to determine which piece to adjust that would possibly move the needle the most, so I could launch it again. And I'll keep re-adjusting until I get the desired result because that's how a success entrepreneur thinks.

Success Disguised in Failure

Here's where it gets interesting... in my past business launches (and there have been many), when I got dismal results like this, I would have felt like such a failure which really sucked! But, what I didn't know back then was... **within every failed attempt exists useful information to guide you toward success!** Truly understanding the depth of this concept is huge... *and* can literally be the difference between *you quitting* or *your inevitable success.*

You see, failure is *not* bad. **But, most of us were *not* trained to view a failed attempt as a step toward success**. But it really is. So, I actually don't think of the Facebook ad launch as a *failure*; I think if it as not yet achieving my target – which is really very different than actually failing. Shifting your mindset to re-frame how you view failed results is a huge step in setting your course for a successful business. Be *prepared* for failed attempts. Don't *focus* on failure, but be prepared for it. Understand that a failed attempt will shine a spotlight on the things you hadn't considered before, thus providing important information for you to make the necessary adjustments to move you toward success.

There's a big distinction here; so it's important to note: **a failed attempt does not make *you* a failure.** Don't take it personally. It's not about *you*. It's simply part of doing business.

When I had a costume manufacturing company, I remember being down to crunch time (that's means the deadline was approaching). And this one particular Renaissance gown just didn't end up looking like I'd imagined it to be. As a matter a fact, it looked really plain and boring. I knew in good conscience, I couldn't just let it go out the door *as is* because it didn't meet the standard of exquisite design for which my company was known. At first I felt like *I'd* failed (because I took it personally). But, then something deep within me rose up to the surface with a knowing there had to be something to fix this situation. I starred at the costume for a while and soon the creative juices began to flow. I grabbed some trim from off the shelf and began pinning it on the gown. With that, I could feel I was onto something good. I spent the next couple of hours attaching various trims in various places. Each trim enhancing the costume's beauty. Then at a certain point, I knew the gown was complete. It was now truly spectacular. And my heart was filled with such joy as I imagined my presentation of this costume to my client. (My client was thrilled beyond belief.)

The most amazing thing is how this gown had been a failure *in my eyes* only hours before. And now it was one of my greatest design accomplishments. The *failed attempt* was actually the catalyst for the spectacular design ideas. After the client picked up the costume, I took some time to think about what had just transpired. And I realized this was not the first time I had a situation like this. I'd experienced many failed attempts that ended up becoming exceptional pieces of work. So it was then, I realized... **there's no such thing as failure. And when my result does not meet my expectation, there's always more creativity inside of me worthy of the challenge.** The truth is, I've truly never had a failure because I've never quit. Instead, I press in with greater focus and with *a trusting* that something great is about to flow from within me... and it always does!

Entrepreneurial DNA

Hello, I'm Wendy Dillard. I'm a serial entrepreneur. I've started many small businesses and have enjoyed quite a number of years earning a good living from my entrepreneurial ventures. And even though from time-to-time, I work in "Corporate," I've always considered myself an Entrepreneur at heart. Corporate experience helps to make me a more well-rounded entrepreneur teaching me much about successful business strategies.

I learned a while back that to understand your true strengths versus weaknesses, **you need to become aware of the things that *energize* you.** A *strength* is an activity that *energizes* you, whereas a *weakness* is an activity that *drains* you.

I can remember years ago (while still awake at 5:00am) reading the IRS tax booklet and thinking to myself, "who does this?" I mean really, who spends their time reading the rules & regulations of business deductions at 5:00am? And the answer would be, *me*! That's just the crazy kind of thing I like to do because being fully immersed in every aspect of successful business life is fun for me.

I get excited & energized whenever I'm engaged in anything that has to do with business. It could be brainstorming new business plans for myself or someone else; or I could be engaged in learning a new technology that will advance my business; or I could be delivering life coaching or business consulting. I love to help others develop their business ideas or share resources that have worked for me. All of these things excite & delight me. And this is why I call myself a serial entrepreneur because these things *energize me to the core of my being* – which is a powerful indicator that being an entrepreneur is a natural strength for me!

I've been asked many times what I do for fun or what my hobbies are... and I feel weird giving the real answer because it's so unusual. What I do for fun is devour books, programs & courses on how businesses become successful. I'm driven to get under-the-hood to learn every facet of a great business model. Yet, I'm just as fascinated by what makes a business fail. There's a plethora to be learned from both favorable & unfavorable results. Understanding how businesses work fascinate me.

The Entrepreneur Mindset Versus the Employee Mindset

In the corporate arena, the CEO, Board of Directors and other upper management are like the architects, managing the vision & steering the direction of the business. And the non-management employees (aka "the worker-bees") are like the construction crew carrying out the architectural blueprints to build and maintain the business. The worker-bees do their specified tasks in exchange for a paycheck.

The role of the Entrepreneur (or Solo-prenuer as it's often referred to when it's just *you* running the business) is a combination of both the Architect & the Worker-Bee. The Solo-preneur has the responsibility of both designing the business plan as well as delivering the product or service. This means, you're responsible for the development of the product or service, brand reputation, administrative stuff, cash-flow, and so much more. An entrepreneur's job is never done. Now, if this sounds like doom & gloom to you, then chances are you don't have an entrepreneurial mindset (and perhaps owning your own business is not really your thing). But, if this sound juicy to you, and it sounds like an exciting adventure, and the only way you want to live, then you naturally have the entrepreneurial spirit!

While working in a corporate job, I recall a conversation with a dear friend & colleague. I was saying how much I looked forwarded to exiting that corporate job and returning to my entrepreneurial roots. And I was shocked at her response. She told me that the thought of being a business owner horrified her. She said she'd never want to leave the safety of a regular paycheck. And in that moment, I realized how she had articulated what the *employee mindset* focuses on... the security of a paycheck.

When you're thinking about going into business for yourself, there's always the consideration of how a new business will be capitalized and/or how quickly will it turn a profit, so it can sustain your lifestyle. But, someone with an *employee mindset* will feel it's too risky to leave the safety of the job to try creating their own business. An employee likes the security of knowing *the company* they work for shoulders the responsible for making sure the paychecks keep coming. Now, an entrepreneur requires income too, but generating an income is not an entrepreneur's primary focus. *A true entrepreneur is focused more on the fun & freedom of being engaged in the business than the financial risk.*

What's interesting to me is that I had always thought *everyone* desired to be an entrepreneur (like I did). And the reason not everyone followed through on their own business had to do with them not knowing how or what to do to build a business. But, it had not occurred to me until I had this conversation with my corporate colleague, that *my* being a serial entrepreneur had *everything* to do with how my mindset was hard-wired and not a matter of know-how.

Even though knowing how to launch a product or service and knowing how to conduct business is an essential aspect of entrepreneurship, the natural inner drive (or mindset) is the primary differentiator between someone that offers their talent & skill in exchange for a paycheck versus the entrepreneur that chooses to market their talent & skill to build their own business.

Let Perfection Go

I read an article about Microsoft that makes an excellent point about how a successful business operates. It said that *if* Microsoft had waited for perfection, they would still not have released their *first* version of their Windows operating system. And if you're a Microsoft user (like I am), you're well aware that *every* version of Windows has bugs upon release, yet they release them anyway. Microsoft understands that once it gets to the marketplace, many customers will be providing feedback helping them to know which changes need to be made. And, even while working on the improvements of their current version of Windows, they are simultaneously working on the design of the next version. **Successful business owners recognize that perfection is not the aim, getting to market *is*.**

Learn to recognize when good enough, *is good enough*, so your product or service can be launched as soon as possible. It doesn't have to be perfect! Because what you really require is for your product or service to get into the hands of your customers. When this happens, you'll receive valuable feedback from your customers. And *their* input gives you specific knowledge of *what* to tweak.

Constant Stream of Ideas

There's something surreal when you launch a new product or service which can be both exhilarating and terrifying. It's like you've put your heart on the line for anyone to possibly stomp on. And simultaneously, you've gifted yourself with an art-form where you get to continually re-mold it and change its form over & over until you're ready to *move on to the next thing*. To be successful in business, whatever idea you've launched into the world *cannot be the last*. **An entrepreneur continually re-invents; it's the call of the entrepreneur.**

When the ideas are flowing fast & furiously, you have to pick a place to focus your attention. And I highly recommend developing *one idea* at a time to keep you from being overwhelmed. But, as soon as your current product or service is launched, it's time to work on the next one to keep the momentum going. Entrepreneurs have more ideas than they'll ever actually launch because they have a never-ending source of innovation. And that's a good thing! But, sometimes the ideas come so fast, it can be overwhelming. And in that case, it can easily prevent an entrepreneur from taking action. So, it's important to be aware that it's *natural* for you to have multiple new ideas flowing at the same time; but be mindful to not let this *paralyze* you into non-action.

A successful entrepreneur needs to have a personal practice of *focus*. I don't know of any entrepreneur that doesn't experience shiny-ball syndrome from time-to-time (or even most of the time). It's in our DNA. But, when you know you've landed on an idea that *feels right*, it's time to *focus* all your attention on that one idea to develop it and get it launched into the marketplace.

Figuring Out the How

I remember when I was deciding if the timing was right to quit my job at a costume company and start freelancing as a costume designer. I wondered if I could earn enough money freelancing. I wasn't really certain, yet deep down, it felt right to me.

My formal education was in *fashion design*, patternmaking & couture sewing skills, so I knew I had a number of skills that were transferable to *costume designing*. But I honestly didn't know if I could masquerade (pun intended) as a costume designer since all I knew about costumes was what I'd picked up during my 4 years at the costume shop, and I wasn't sure if that was sufficient. And honestly while at that shop, I often felt like a fish out of water as clients & colleagues would talk in great detail about costumes found in classic plays & musicals. And when they wanted to pull me into the conversation, I would do a bit of linguistic song & dance to give the impression I knew what I was talking about (when I really hadn't a clue). So I wondered, if I freelanced, would I know enough to get by in the world of costuming.

And as much as my gut said to "go for it" – I was still concerned I wouldn't be able to pull it off without my costume buddies by my side. So, I decided to have a heart-to-heart conversation with my costume colleague & friend. I knew he had freelanced prior to coming to this costume shop, so I asked for his advice. And here is what he told me... he said that if a potential client asked if I could do XYZ, and I had no idea how to do XYZ – he told me to *confidently* reply, "Yes I can do that." And then he said, "*and then it's your job to figure it out.*"

In my 10 years of freelancing as a costume designer, I did said *"yes"* to everything that came my way - regardless if I knew how I would pull it off. Sometimes, that meant I called my costuming friend for his advice, or sometimes I found a costume book that answered my questions, or I found something else that got me over the hurdle. And once I did it, I could add that to my resume! His words of wisdom were truly some of the best entrepreneurial advice I'd ever been given. And even though I've left costuming, I continue to use that advice in whatever business arena in which I'm playing.

So, even if an entrepreneur doesn't know *how* to do an aspect of business, it's important to recognize its part of the job to learn *how*. This is another key concept that every entrepreneur wants to have rooted solidly in their mindset. **Not knowing *how* to do something should not be a deterrent to doing business, *instead consider it "on-the-job training."***

Follow the Fun Factor

For me, freelancing as a costume designer and then opening a costume manufacturing company fulfilled me professionally & personally in every way, shape & form for many years. But, when it stopped being fun for me and I no longer felt personally fulfilled by it, I knew it was time to exit that business. And so, I retired from costuming. I know it was the right decision because I've never looked back and don't miss it at all. And with that, it was time to consider what else was possible that could bring me fun!

Take-Aways

You Know You Have an Entrepreneurial Mindset If...

- When you think about business ideas (or are working in your business), *you're energized* (versus feeling drained). Of course, you might feel mentally and/or physically tired after doing good work, but it's a *good tired* where you feel a deep sense of accomplishment.

- You're more focused on the fun & freedom that the business creates than the financial risk.

- You continually have a steady stream of new business ideas flowing.

Three Powerful Entrepreneurial Beliefs...

- There's no such thing as failure; there's only feedback because within every failed attempt exists useful information to guide you toward success.

- Entrepreneurs don't allow *perfection* to stall or stop a good idea from being launched because they know when to recognize when good enough, *is good enough.*

- Not knowing how to do something *is the catalyst for figuring it out.*

You know you have the Entrepreneurial Mindset when the only thing that feels right is being in your own business... living life on your terms!

The Author

Wendy Dillard
www.CreatingBusinessBeyondThisReality.com/wendy-dillard

CHAPTER 17

Business Becca's Way; Exploration of an Entrepreneur

BECCA SPEERT

$\mathbf{M}$y search for a means to support myself was merely a small part of my greater search for direction, a concept of purpose, and a sense of self. I was a born seeker, constantly searching for more. Entrepreneurship was inevitable for me. Here I share with you some of the details of how I got to where I am today in hopes that it will entertain the established, and encourage the explorers.

As children, many of us were asked to consider what we would like to *be* when we grew up, as if our intended profession was going to pave our way to adulthood. I did not have a solid answer like many of the other kids did. The question had me unsettled and I preferred to be the one asking questions. What if for some of us, the reverse was more suitable? What if our personalities and natural strengths could shape our career? What if our innate abilities could be the marketable item? To this day, I still spend most of my time asking questions, of myself, and my clients.

Success eventually follows passion

During my formative years, I was fortunate enough to find myself in environments that were suited to exploration and personal discovery. As the years went by, my brain demanded more intellectual stimulation. I bounced between many jobs and changed my degree more than a handful of times. In high school, I enrolled in extra curricular art classes when I realized that I could not only skip gym class, but I could also get free periods to extend my lunchtime or sleep in extra hours in the morning. I have very supportive parents that saw my passion for the arts and allowed me to do this. I spent summers during high school in the Berkshires of Massachusetts blowing glass, spinning pottery, and dying fabrics. The freedom to choose my own activities and schedule them into my education, to my advantage, set the stage for how I do business today.

During the school year my mom would shuttle me from the suburbs to evening glassblowing classes in Boston and Worcester. The more art classes I went to, the more free periods I had to spend time doing things like sleeping in, hiking in the woods, and playing Frisbee with my friends. The more fun I was having, the less I was motivated to go to class.

My father, recognizing that I needed to be tricked into finishing high school, strategically encouraged me to apply to art schools, reminding me that it would require that I graduate. His technique worked! I graduated high school that spring (just barely), and was able to enter as a freshman at Virginia Commonwealth University that Fall. VCU was not a good fit, but with actual interest in the course material, I excelled. That year I learned a whole lot more about who I was, how I functioned, and what I desired. When the school year concluded in the spring of 2003, I moved back home to calculate my next move.

Allowing others to see you and receiving their contribution

Back in high school, my father knew what was motivating to me and instead of forcing me toward an assumed lucrative academic track, he guided me toward my strength.

During the spring of 2003, I began to experience chronic pain all over my body. In order to stay close to home and my doctors, I continued college locally at the University Of Massachusetts Amherst. After a year and a half of studying geology, I registered for an elective called Sustainable Living with Dr. John Gerber in the Plant and Soil Science Department. Gerber was the first educator that reassured me that nothing was wrong with me and like my father, he acknowledged and nurtured my strengths.

UMass had a huge campus, and by the time John and I met, my pain had grown worse and walking to my classes was a challenge. I acquired a handicap placard so that I could easily drive door to door. Sitting for long periods of time was also extremely uncomfortable, and this made attending lectures difficult for me. Instead of miserably sitting in the cramped lecture hall chairs, I spoke up to one of the teaching assistants and requested that she bring in a table and chair. Leaning on the table for support during class and sitting upright made a huge difference for me. John got word of this and commended me for my willingness to acknowledge my needs and ask for accommodation.

John was extremely supportive during one of the hardest times of my life. He encouraged me to be myself without apology and communicated to me that by doing so I was an inspiration for others, inviting them to do the same. After I completed his course, he invited me back to be a teaching assistant and co-facilitate an honors section for his next round of students. I was thrilled to accept.

During my time at UMass, I was battling all sorts of physical issues, and I didn't stop seeking a solution. As my physical problems got worse, I ended up leaving the Geology department and transferred to the Bachelor's Degree of Individual Concentration department (BDIC). BDIC offers self-directed students the opportunity to design their own majors in collaboration with advisors. Dr. John Gerber agreed to be my advisor. It was a lot of extra time and effort to create my curriculum and get approval for each class, but it was worth it. My body discomfort was at an all time person high (geology course work was proving to be physically demanding) and I liked the idea of only choosing classes based on my specific interests. I didn't mind the extra effort if it meant I could take any class that I desired. I completed a minor in geology, and created a Bachelor's of Art Degree that I labeled "Environmental and Cultural Sustainability." I did not have a clear picture of what I could do with the degree, but I was studying what fed my curiosity and suited my personality, and I knew that the rest would follow.

Studying what I was passionate about did not qualify me for a traditional job, but it made a huge difference in my academic performance and set the foundation for my diverse coaching practice today. I barely passed my classes in high school, but by the end of college in 2008, I had made the dean's list every semester and graduated cum laude. Even if a situation looks dire, with passion, commitment, and drive it has an enormous opportunity to get better, and the worse it is, the more room there is for improvement!

Still Seeking

I worked many jobs during and after college; I apprenticed with shamans (indigenous healers), worked for organic farms, interned with a non-profit that advocated for the human rights of sweatshop workers, I served on the board for the Amherst Fair Trade Coalition, coordinated activities at both a nursing home and an elementary after school program, worked as a barista, and volunteered at a permaculture design firm and an outdoors homeschool program for children. I was covering my bases: holistic health, art, environmentalism, and social justice.

In 2010, I applied to the Conway School of Landscape Design: a prestigious ecology and sustainability focused graduate design program. While I was nervously waiting for their reply, I was considering what else I would like to do if I was not accepted. During my research, I came across a permaculture and wilderness skills program for adults (Regenerative Design and Nature Awareness Essentials "RDNA"). By the time I received my admittance letter, I had come to realize that I could not design sustainable landscapes with integrity unless I had the experience like that of the RDNA program first. Potentially, I could be heading toward another dead-end and wondered if I was making the best decision, but I wanted to learn more about ecology and living in harmony with the land before modifying it professionally. I was going to learn to track animals, understand bird language and behavior, and experience the environment hands on. To me, it seemed that should be required for anyone potentially disrupting sensitive ecosystems. That is what I told myself, to rationalize my decision. I had decided; I was California bound.

We camped on the coastline three days a week, together as a village, and dispersed to our own lives the rest of the time. During my program off-days, I waitressed in the mornings, serving omelets, po' boys, and beignets, and in the evenings I enjoyed gardening at home in my backyard oasis. On most days, RDNA had us up at dawn, some mornings crawling on hands and knees through frozen dew covered meadows to watch the birds and observe predator disturbances. At other times we experimented with homesteading, food production, landscape design, installations of different waste removal systems, story telling, and learning survival skills. At night we would gather around a fire and share stories of the day, before winding down in our tents for the night. Living outside three days a week made for a very exciting year.

Making the most of it

My health grew worse during the program and since I was in a hub of alternative medicine, I consulted with several naturopaths. The assessments and recommendations that I received sent my head spinning, so instead of taking their word for it, I enrolled in the Institute For Integrative Nutrition; the world's largest nutrition school and certification program. There was an herbalist in town that agreed to let me take her classes in exchange for designing her an educational demonstration garden in a public park nearby, for growing and harvesting herbs.

Although in pain and not able to work full time, I continued to develop my skills as actively as I could, in the midst of trying to heal. I worked for a non-profit educating children about climate change, began apprenticing to become a birth doula, and amongst it all, I crossed paths with a woman who insisted that she ordain me as a Priestess (why not?). I was adding more and more to my repertoire, still uncertain where it was leading me professionally.

I knew people back home were wondering what I was going to do to make a substantial living when I stopped taking all of these certificate programs. There was no answer yet, but I was following what excited me and prioritizing my health -I didn't see any other way.

The graduate program had allowed me to defer for one year, but one year had passed and my interest had shifted elsewhere. I continued to question what my next step would be.

What could give me the freedom I desired, without the limitations of a traditional job, and include all the sectors of my interests while utilizing my medley of skills?

In 2012 I launched a private holistic health and life coaching practice that I named HealthRoots. I loved working with my clients, witnessing their success was rewarding and their feedback was touching, but it was not bringing in the income I had hoped for.

Taking Leaps!

My time in California had run its course and I was eager to head back east. While I was planning my move, dōTERRA essential oils turned up. I was turned off that it was network marketing so I said no to a couple of representatives who approached me with the business proposition before I finally purchased a customer membership. At the time, I was going through an emotionally tumultuous period and my body and my mind needed something drastic.

I started using the dōTERRA products and not only did they soothe my body, they also dramatically changed my life. The muscle relief rub eliminated muscle and tendon pain I had had for years. The discomfort dissipated overnight, like I took a magic pill. I ditched my nightly sleeping remedy with four drops of a blend of calming essential oils. Something new had stolen my curiosity! It was clear that they were highly effective, and I had to explore them more, but at this point of my life I was still refusing to "sell" anything.

Halfway back while driving to the East Coast I decided to take a job offer in Lawrence, Kansas to work as a weight loss consultant at a corporate weight loss clinic. I thought if I worked for someone else it would be easier and I would make more money. At the time, with the choices I had, I liked the idea of consistent income and what I thought was going to be consistent clientele. That mirage quickly faded. Business was slow, and there was little room to make a difference for people. There was an incredible potential for improvement, but when I began developing holistic nutrition and positive mindset programs for my clients, my manager wrote me up and reported me to the corporate office. I was not following the rules to stick to their formula. They explained to me that I was being paid [hourly, plus commission] to sell their supplements/programs and make cold calls to prospective and previous clients, not to improve conditions for their clients.

After my job was threatened, I followed the rules and got really good at selling their supplements, while seeing private HealthRoots clients and consulting for dōTERRA on my own time. The more I learned about the essential oils, the more frustrating it became to keep my mouth shut at the weight loss center. For every case I handled, I knew a cheaper, safer, more effective dōTERRA product that would solve their problem and it was driving me crazy. If I were going to sell anything at all, I preferred that it would be something that would nurture people's bodies while being kind to the environment.

I was miserable at my job and had dōTERRA staring me in the face, ready to fly. Here was a brand that I knew well, had the values I was looking for, and had an exceptional compensation plan. The time had come to quit my job, so I put in my two weeks notice, got organized, and started teaching classes. I got out in public and attended sustainable professional networking events. I would listen to people complain about what was bothering them and approach them with questions, then invite those that were interested to try free samples. I loved hearing people's successes, I loved being of service to people, and I loved that I could make my own hours, travel, socialize, and be a part of a company I was proud of.

Business My Way

At first I rebelled against the network marketing system. I hated the idea of following a template and doing the same thing over and over again. After a while I was convinced by a couple of colleagues to give the formula a try. My business did accelerate, but the repetition wore me out. Eventually, I went back to doing things my way again, but I incorporated some of the new tools and strategies that I had learned and saw were beneficial. My business continued to grow, and people wanted to know my tricks. It was hard to convey at first because it came so naturally. I would answer them with things like "Well, I just go to networking events" or "I listen to hear what people complain about." It was so instinctive for me, that I didn't realize what I knew was not obvious to others, and how much detail I was actually leaving out.

When a skill comes naturally to us, we can unknowingly overlook it and take it for granted. Those gifts become a marketable product required by the individuals who lack it. Suited clients will be happy to employ us because the job is done skillfully, and we get paid for doing what we love.

What comes so naturally to you that it takes no effort?

What is so much fun for you that you would do for nothing if money were not an issue?

There lie the possibilities for a fulfilling, successful business.

It is not all about the money

One of the things that come naturally to me is connecting with people, and creating mutually beneficial relationships. Wherever I move to or travel through, I run into and build connections with the healers, the academics, the seekers, the land stewards, and the connectors just like me. I become privy to the best of the best in my circles.

This may not generate cash, per se, but I am in my element, which is empowering and enjoyable, and generates a web of future collaborations and possibilities. I love helping others when they need a referral, and I find gratification supporting other business people to thrive.

I find pleasure in the process and when I am contributing to other people's success, it gifts right back to me. Referral networks are a beautiful thing.

What networks can you tap into?

What can you do that gives you the opportunity to be in your element while creating possibilities for the future?

Despite your logical mind, follow your curiosity

In the Nature Awareness movement, the "child's mind" refers to approaching tasks and ideas with total curiosity, as if your mind was a blank slate.

Over the past years my curiosity has led me to all sorts of experiences with crafts, art, sustainable farming, nature awareness, holistic medicine, non-violent communication, ceremonial work, and so much more. It may have seemed random to the onlooker, or even to me, but all of it fed parts of me, and have ended up contributing to me in one way or another.

The universe is a mysterious place. When you honor yourself and follow your curiosity instead of doing everything in a certain order, people and circumstances can seem to emerge at the most opportune moments, and ones that no longer contribute to you will fall away. If you are sentimental like me this can sometimes cause heartache and worry, but later on you can see why you were better of without that person/job/opportunity. People who will negatively impact your path may become difficult to deal with, leave you, or become unreachable. Ones that resonate with you will come into your life. People may come in and out depending on when it aligns. A certain flow generates when you function from this space of creation. Do not doubt what inspires, and do not apologize for being you, but become aware of the rhythms around you and perceive what is really happening. Enjoy the experiences and people that resonate with where you are at in your development, but do not take them for granted.

It never shows up the way you think it will show up

One of the discoveries I have made over the years is that my body is one of my greatest allies for awareness. A body picks up on things that the mind has not yet become privy to. That is why our "gut feeling" can often be spot-on. Our bodies can feel spacious or contracted as a way of tapping into the energy about something, and then our brains kick in next to analyze that which we have already experienced, something we are experiencing, or something that someone else has experienced-the later is typically valued more.

We can tune into our body for information and receive the awareness if we recognize it before letting our logic kick in. This can be done by literally asking a question directed at our body and observing the first thought or sensation that arises. We can also talk to our projects and ask our business for information, then allow ourselves to perceive how our body responds, or notice if an instant awareness pops up. It may sound crazy, but the more you practice this, the more you will start to conduct business from a place of instantaneous "knowing" instead of thinking it through. Yep, you can develop, or uncover psychic abilities that you have had all along. It gets easier with repetition, and I promise you that when you get the hang of it, it will be far simpler and effective than functioning purely from reason every time. Incorporating this visceral style of decision-making employs less overall effort and gives us the opportunity to function based on both intelligence and awareness.

During recent decades, so many of us have clogged our bodies up with processed foods, environmental pollution, and inundation with electronic and social stimuli that simplifying what we eat, put on our body, and surround ourselves with, can also contribute to enhancing these abilities. When I work with clients to clean up their diet, the quality of their self-care products, and their daily habits, they always become more sensitive and more aware as a result.

Deep Listening

My business changes and shifts, and every day is different. There is some structure, but I do allow it to take on a certain life of it's own, not only because it is more fun that way, but because things can take on a certain flow, that my micormanaging can hinder.

When someone cancels at the last minute, instead of indulging in frustration, I like to ask *"what can I better use this hour for?"* or something similar. I will either get an idea right away, it gives me the extra time I needed for a fast approaching deadline, someone else will call me that I needed to connect with, or something else serendipitous happens. It can be quite entertaining and is much easier than getting upset.

Another question that I invite you to give a shot if you are wanting direction is *"What needs my attention right away?"* or *"What can I accomplish today?"* Open ended questions like this can result in you having an idea of what task will be the most productive first, and then you can continue asking more questions to guide you throughout the day. This keeps you productive, without enforcing too much limitation. They key is to avoid overruling your awareness with logic.

Timing with business (and everywhere for that matter), is a factor that many people do not grasp entirely. A lot of my clients think that to be more productive, they must work harder, faster, or longer. On the contrary, if we use timing to our advantage and place our attention where it is required (following our awareness), we can often see better results by simply taking breaks from certain tasks and giving the area of focus time to breathe. Sometimes switching from one project to another, or choosing leisure, despite that seemingly not making any sense, is precisely what can help to generate momentum behind the scenes. It is not about linearity, it is about energetic flow.

For example, maybe you have a flash of a thought to go to a coffee shop in a neighborhood nowhere near your house, but you have plans to de-clutter your filing cabinet. You have plenty of coffee at home, why would you go clear across town and waste precious time when you have so much to do? Now that you are keeping an eye out for fleeting awarenesses, you realize this may be worth entertaining, so you go. When you arrive to the coffee shop, someone strikes up a conversation with you who becomes a new client, you run into a friend you have not seen in years, or end up meeting a professional organizer that you can hire to tackle your files! We can not always foresee exactly how things will turn out, but when we let go and follow what feels light, circumstances tend to be far more of a contribution than if we micromanaged every moment of the day, and every segment of our business.

Money can't make you happy, but happiness can make you money!

Think beyond cash, consider money as abundance in all of its forms: Money = cash, material goods, free experiences, abundance and flow in mind/body/physicality and what else?

You may be wondering how money follows happiness, and I will remind you that all things interact energetically. First, let us consider the reverse. "Murphy's Law" is the concept that "anything that can go wrong, will go wrong." When someone is seeing life through that lens, it is challenging *not* to experience life as a series of unfortunate events. If someone is depressed, it can be a struggle to surf the flow of life with ease. Of course, as with anything it is not simply either or, and you may question which came first, the chicken or the egg, however, a vibrant joyful person often traverses challenges with a grace and ease and that can foster more desirable results.

You may be thinking "Well yeah, easy for you to say. If you are broke, your life is not going to be easy, and it takes time and resources to change it." I will respond by asking, what if it was not about forcing change, but asking for something else to show up? Below I will share some simple questions to ask that can begin to shift the energy. If someone is functioning from a place of genuine happiness, joy, and experiencing the pleasure of being simply being alive, he/she is already receiving a certain abundance of energy from the universe and open to receiving more from life (that includes money!).

Whether you hate your job or are excited to go to work every day, you can benefit from asking these questions:

"What is fun for me and what can I do to add more of that to my life?"

"What will it take to expand my willingness to receive today?"

"What is fun and easy for me to do (that others seem to have a harder time with?)" *Market those skills!*

"If time and money were not an issue, what kind of job would I like to have?"

"If I could have more than one job, what other jobs would I like to have?

"If I never had to stop learning, what would I study?"

"What more can I contribute to the world by just being me?"

Retrospect

Looking back now, I see how every twist and turn, every challenge, and every bout of seemingly poor timing supported my evolution. My mode of operation had originally been impulse and I was acting on emotions while grappling with logic. It is obvious to me now, where I resisted the flow of my life, and yet, it is how I got where I am today. There are no wrong decisions, just choices that give us more awareness if we pay attention.

In the past I had been hard on myself if I was not earning as much cash as my other financially stable compadres, but I have always had a home to live in, enough food to eat, clothes to wear, travel fare, etc. Even if I did not purchase all of it with money I earned from my job, I have been receiving it nonetheless. Practicing gratitude not only gives you perspective, but keeps your energy open to receiving more.

What abundance have you received that you have not acknowledged yet?

Would you be willing to qualify that as wealth and take a new inventory?!

What if you never had to figure out your next step?

A small shift in perspective can create immense change in your inner and outer world.

There is no expectation for you to take my word for any of this. If you are inspired to experiment with these concepts, please do. They cannot hurt, and you might be delightfully surprised with the effects. Live your life, lean into the projects that are fun for you, engage when the flow is easy, and apply your skills where they produce the most.

Today, I coach clients with a variety of tools that I would never have acquired had I not followed what inspired me. *What gift can you be to the world when you follow what inspires you?*

I invite you quiet the monkey mind, ask some questions, let go of your timeline, entertain your curiosities, do what is fun for you, let the universe deliver, and enjoy the surprises when things show up ever better than your brain could have designed.

If you feel excited at all right now, you are aligning with these concepts. This energy is surfacing because you are far more capable of doing joyful business, outside of this reality, than you have ever acknowledged.

The Author

Becca Speert

www.CreatingBusinessBeyondThisReality.com/becca-speert

What I Wish I'd Known Before I Started, but Probably Wouldn't Have Listened to Anyway

KALI LANE

Your Vision is Key

For years I got tastes of what my business could be. Every once in a while, I would tap into this massive, expansive energy that totally lit me up. Then I would go back to being caught up in day-to-dayness of work. That expansive energy just felt like a fantasy to me. I had thought of it as a possibility, but not as something I could actually create.

I thought it was all in my head, just a picture. I had lived my life from fantasy – fantasizing about all the things I wished I had, fantasizing about the perfect life and everything that went with it. That's what we do, right? We are taught to imagine. But we are not taught to create. What I didn't realize was that that "fantasy" was my vision and it was asking to be created.

You *know* what you would like to create, have and be. You know it because those are the things that light you up, turn you on, and expand your being. It is the things that bring peace, the softness of vulnerability, and the intensity of a potency you know deep in your being.

What is it that you desire to create in the world and in your own life? No matter how big or small you think it is, whether you think it is something world-changing or just something fun you'd like to do, what is it? What do you love about it? What is the energy of it? That is what your "vision" or "aim" is and you can create it.

Choice, Commitment and Action

How many people do you know who talk about all of the things they want to be or do, but never do them? Most of them? What is that? Are they lazy? Do they not have the talent or skills to do those things?

What if it is that the majority of us didn't grow up learning how to create? We are taught how to do numbers and letters and we learn about stuff that happened in the past – but what about how to create the future? What about the life skills that don't focus on a specific skill or trade, but that can facilitate you in any trade? The stuff that can allow you to create *anything*?

Choice is something we don't learn here. We are taught right and wrong and how to make decisions. We've been taught to find the right and final answer so we can catalogue it and always make the right and perfect choice.

But does it work?

Needing to have the right point of view and make the right decision can be immobilizing. Have you ever gone into "choice paralysis" because you didn't know what the right decision was? Many people have so many conflicting points of view that they've taken on from others, that trying to find the "right" path or take the "right" step ends with them making no choice at all.

Choice is different than decision. You don't have to judge to choose. You don't have to judge what is wrong in order to choose the "right" thing. You don't have to cut yourself off from any other possibilities. You just choose.

If you aren't immobilizing yourself with perpetual judgment, creating a lifetime of indecision, you have access to something you didn't before – commitment.

Commitment is wholehearted. It's the unwavering, full-bodied essence of being the choice, which allows everything else to fall away in support of the creation of your choice.

Commitment doesn't mean you choose one thing and now you can't ever choose again. Your choice isn't being taken away, your awareness isn't being diminished. When you make a choice you will get the energy of what that choice will create. If you are only half-choosing, wavering, going back and forth trying to figure out the right choice, you probably won't get that far. You *can* know what your choice will create. How many reasons, justifications and judgments do you have to have in order to make a decision and stick with it no matter what? With choice, if you want to choose something different in 10 seconds, you can commit to that choice, too.

What are you committed to right now? This reality? Waiting for everyone else to get on board so you don't leave them behind? Not being judged? Judging yourself?

If you were fully committed to your life, what would that create?

So you make a choice, truly step in and commit. And then you get this expansive energy. What now? Take action. This is another piece that we often don't do here. It's so nice to fantasize about all of the cool things we want – but it feels *really* different to actually take action toward them. Then it's real. It's not just a fantasy in your head. Its real life and you're in it. If you don't take action, you will complete the fantasy in your head, which will, in turn, satisfy your craving for it and make you not want to take action. Funny how that works, huh?

Your request is what the universe responds to. What you are actualizing in your life is created based on your asks, your demands and your choices. Sometimes things show up seemingly out of nowhere without you having to lift a finger. Sometimes it actually requires you to *do* something. If you are trying to build your coaching business, you might want to answer that phone call from a client. If you are creating an organization, it might be more generative to file that paperwork than to avoid it. If you truly desire something to show up, you have to *choose* it and then take the necessary actions.

Your Choice Will Get You Farther than Talent or Ability Alone

Is there something you have a talent for? That is a great thing to offer as a service! There are probably things that come so easy to you that you dismiss them entirely. Maybe you don't see them as valuable, maybe you don't even recognize them. It is easy to disregard your natural capacities because they seem normal to you, but not everyone shares the same capacities. Are you good at organizing? Do you have a knack for teaching or love sharing what you have learned? Do you love talking to people? Are you constantly connecting people? Your talents are things you can do with ease, that would be a contribution to people who don't do them easily, and you could make money doing them. Just some food for thought, if you are unsure where you'd like to go.

What do you do when you *don't* think you're good at what you would like to do?

When I was in massage school, people always said I had "healing hands." It is easy to latch onto things that people say you are good at. I wasn't interested in just doing relaxation massages, though. During my second year of massage school, I learned Forceline Theory, a treatment-focused deep tissue designed for pain relief. It wasn't just learning how to make people feel good, I had to learn how to figure out what was going on in the body. Why did this client have low back pain? If two clients had similar symptoms, why did one get better and the other didn't? People still liked my touch, but this was a whole new ball game. I didn't feel smart or knowledgeable enough to do treatment.

While I was trying to memorize nerve pathways, biomechanical laws and treatment protocols, some of the other students were already connecting the dots, asking assessment questions beyond our discussion, and I didn't even know how they'd gotten there. For my first few years as a massage therapist, I felt like I was just applying my best formula-based guesses: This Symptom = That Protocol.

I felt lucky that I had learned some great protocols, because I got decent results. But when I didn't (or when decent wasn't enough), I didn't know *why*, or what else to look for. And because I hadn't thought I was smart enough to figure it out, I never tried. At least, not for a while. I got burnt out, took a break from massage and when I started again, everything changed.

I started taking classes again, learning new modalities, learning more treatment. If my default protocols with my clients weren't working, I would try something different. I didn't know what it would create, but I learned piece by piece how to connect the dots. I learned to recognize more, work more efficiently, and get better and better results. Why? *Because I kept choosing to.*

No matter what you want to learn or how far you want to go, it is all just choice. If you keep choosing it, and choosing based on the energy, you will get there or even somewhere greater. Don't worry about the people you think are better than you, because do you know what I have learned? Most people stop. Because I didn't stop when I felt defeated, or stupid, or less than, I learned that if you just keep choosing, you will get there. The reason most people don't is because they don't choose it. It is all too easy to get to a nice, comfortable place and stop learning, stop creating, stop changing, and stop growing.

This is one of the reasons that comparisons don't work. In the end, it doesn't matter whether someone seems to have a natural talent for something or be better than you at something. Someone could have a natural talent and not do anything with it. Someone else could choose to do it anyway, and create something great.

And if you choose the "what am I good at" route, you will *still* have to choose it.

There is No Right Answer, a.k.a. Do What Works for You

There is no right answer, only what you would like to create.

I spent years not wanting to make a wrong move. Creating a treatment-focused massage practice and being in the public eye was daunting. In addition to not being "good enough" at treatment, I didn't understand business; it was a whole world I didn't identify with. I felt like some girl "playing business," like a kid playing house. I looked for the right answer to everything. Was I doing the "right" kind of bodywork? When I did finally choose to expand my business, would I be the "right" kind of employer?

The thing is, none of it is right. It is all just choice. What works for you? What works for your business?

I got to the point where, if I got stuck with a client, I wouldn't just give up or refer them out. I would go in with them for a session with my instructor from school. I could have easily sent them over by themselves, but I knew that if I went with them I would get an hour of training on something specific that I was having trouble with. That is not a typical business practice, but it worked for me.

Talking about it to a massage therapist friend of mine even inspired her to do the same when she got stuck and, between the two of us, we ended up convincing the instructor to teach a class. You might not know exactly what something is going to create, but you do know what is going to work for you. Even if you only do it once and learn it is something that you wouldn't choose again, you still have more awareness.

Stop looking for the right business to have, the right way to do business, the right way to do *anything*. It's all choice.

You Can Think Your Way into an Image, but BEing Creates Persona

I had so many judgments about my business. My head was filled with what a massage therapist was supposed to be like, what the treatments should be like, how my business should look...

I didn't realize that none of it was true. It is all just an *interesting point of view*. Some of "my" points of view came from other people. Some were the based on what I'd seen. Most came from my own insecurities. I was trying to create an image of a business owner and treatment specialist.

If you try to create your business from image, you are creating it from judgment (and *other people's* points of view), which decreases your awareness. Being and creating what works for you is persona. It is attractive, inviting, personable and vulnerable. From that space of being, not only will you create a business that works for you, but your contribution to your business will be greater. You will be able to perceive what it requires and create it as *it* desires.

Now what I choose isn't based on how I think it will look. I choose based on what it will create. What keeps showing up in my business? What works and what doesn't? What is streamlined and what isn't? What is going to make doing business with me as easy as possible for my clients? It is a process of continual expansion.

Your Business is Dynamic

Are you looking for the perfect business model? Or wondering what your business will look like and how it will function when it is all finished? If you are looking for the end result of your business, stop. You won't find the perfect business model or ideal image of what your business looks like and then just get to sit back and zone out. Your business isn't something that finishes.

If you are looking for the finish line, you will kill your business. You might be able to force it into existence with some dashes of creation, expansion, and possibility thrown in here and there, but what happens at the finish line? The race is over. It's an end. If you are looking for the end product, you might be able to create it, but you may also create that as the limitation of your business.

What I didn't realize in becoming an entrepreneur is that change would be my new M.O. Every time I tried to stop or check out, I would see my practice slow down. Every time I would finally change something that had been stagnating and bugging me for a while, I would see it grow and become more vibrant again.

Honestly, if I had known how much I would have to pay attention to my business in order for it to work, I might not have done it in the first place. But I'll tell you what, continuing to create and contribute to your business and to change what isn't working, takes *far* less effort than trying to avoid something into existence. If you are already trying to ignore or force aspects of your business, *you are doing it the hard way. It gets easier.*

As you grow, you will change. As you meet your goals, you will grow beyond them. There will always be more and that's a good thing. If you are not one of those people who can find "their thing," settle down and be content with it, then you are going to have to get used to always desiring more. That means change will be *your* M.O. Own it, love it, and creation will be your new reality.

You Know What is Required

Knowing what is required in your business is *far* simpler than it seems. If you are functioning from the polarity of right and wrong, it can be daunting. If you are trying to choose based on right and wrong, your choices are based on judgment. It is never easy because there are so many conflicting points of view.

I have worked with business coaches and read tons of books on various self-help and how-to topics, business and otherwise. It is easy for me to completely lose myself in whatever method or philosophy presented because someone else seems so sure of it.

So how *do* you know? How do you begin to know what you know? I bet there are a ton of things you already do know!

What lights you up?

This goes back to your "vision," but is the same with smaller things, too. Are there things that pop into your awareness and just light you up? Yes, listen to those. That could be the energy of what it would create if you chose it.

Listen to the whispers.

Remember that, while judgments are loud, your awareness is quiet. Awareness often comes in fleeting wisps and whispers. Judgments and opinions tend to hang around for a while.

If you are having trouble hearing the whispers, try getting quiet. When my mind is full of chatter or I am stressed out about the several dozen things on my list, it is easy to keep shoving my awareness aside. Feeling like I can't take a break or slow down (or breathe) is a perfect indicator that I might need that break – from the shoulds, have tos and can'ts. It's not necessarily about the time or how busy you are, it's about stepping out of judgment. When you are the space of being, the whispers aren't so quiet.

What isn't working or where are you using too much effort?

If I am spending too much time, expending too much effort, or when things just seem difficult, I know that something has to change. There is always more possible than you think there is.

After years of owning my own practice, I started the process of expansion... for the second time. I quit the first time. I committed the second time. In less than a year, I have seen more change in myself and in my business than in the previous three years. It never shows up the way you think it will. I could now see where I desired to go, but the tangible day-to-day things in my business seemed to be going backwards. I didn't understand what was happening.

I had started to dial in my vision and make sure that I was choosing was in alignment with it. The more I tried to fine tune it, the more I would see what wasn't working. The dissonance between what could be created and what was impeding it was staggering.

I was having trouble getting across what I actually do. People kept coming in looking for full-body relaxation massages. So, I made sure I started explaining what to expect from the deep tissue and how it was different, but the explanations that had always worked before weren't working anymore. I began to realize how much information I was *not* giving, how much I thought my explanation implied, but never got across. No wonder they didn't know what to expect.

I had an opportunity to look at what was wasn't working and what was required. I started having different conversations with my clients. I took the opportunity to give them the missing pieces of information during their sessions. Then I thought of ways I could answer their questions before they even booked an appointment. I wrote blogs with the information and changed the website to direct them there. It helped a little bit, but not enough. Instead of just having the information on the website, why not have a physical handout they can take home with them? All of these things are simple and they are born from acknowledging what isn't working and simply doing something different.

You will get more awareness with each change. Explaining the difference between Swedish Massage and Deep Tissue in the first place, then changing the explanation when that wasn't enough. Making the information more accessible by putting it on the website, making it even more accessible by handing it to them directly. Each choice will get you closer and will create more awareness.

You really do know. You don't have to know everything and it will continue to change and be refined. It doesn't have to be perfect. Even when you think you've dialed in your systems to the max, you will continue to grow and expand and so will your business.

All of these aspects can be dialed down to recognizing what you would like to create, choosing it, and continuing to keep choosing. Reality isn't as real as you think it is. You don't have to try to find the "right" anything. You really *do* know what works, and you have the power to choose whatever you want. Your choice is a huge contribution and if you choose to create your own reality, you can go beyond the one you know now.

The Author

Kali Lane

www.CreatingBusinessBeyondThisReality.com/kali-lane

CHAPTER 19

Creating Success with a Yoga Mind

ANDORA FREEDOM

"Blessed are the weird people: poets, misfits, writers
mystics, painters, troubadours for they teach us to see the
world through different eyes."
– Jacob Nordby

W̲ho are you? Who are you beyond the face you
show everyone out there? What is it that makes up your deepest desires and your why for everything you do in life? What are the parts
of you that you work so hard to hide and what would your life be like
if you chose to be all that you truly be?

The ancient Greeks inscribed, "Know thyself" in the forecourt of the
Temple of Apollo at Delphi, for it is from this deep knowing that all
great wisdom flows. When we live life from this place of deep knowing, we can easily tap into the potency of the universe and life flows
with grace and ease. Without it, life is seemingly full of challenge,
hardship, confusion and loss.

I've spent many years in the yoga world through my own practice and teaching as well as founding and owning one of the nation's most renowned yoga centers. The first of the ancient Yoga Sutras written by Patanjali reads, "Atha Yoga Anushasanam" and it means "Yoga begins now". The importance of this is that yoga or union with the divine and every part of divine creation, which is what I believe every human is ultimately seeking, is available to each of us every moment and with every breath. It's simply up to us to choose it.

When I was young I was pretty lost. I didn't get life on this planet. Once I reached high school, I tried to find a way to fit in. I was not among the popular girls because I was awkward and terribly shy. At that time there was this art teacher who was beautiful, creative and full of life. I remember her as being such a bright light among many who seemed to be lost or asleep moving through life like sheep. I wanted to spend time with her until I heard a friend tell me how weird this teacher was and all the others chimed in and laughed. My character was weak back then. Little did I understand at that time that it is better to be the rare bird that is bizarre, weird, different, if that is who you truly are rather than trying to squeeze yourself into a mold that has nothing to do with who you truly are, but is accepted by many. That was the beginning of my choosing to dim my own light in order not to shine too bright and then possibly be shamed, made fun of or disliked by others. My greatest fear, as it is for many is not being loved and cared for. This is a basic human need that we all require in order to survive and thrive and thus it is a deep fear that most of us carry. In order to try and fulfill this need from others I chose to turn away from myself and that was the beginning of a very long road filled with gobs of nasty bumps with different stories, but the same pattern underneath it all. The crazy thing is, maybe my "weird" is exactly what the world needs most and the thing that would bring me the greatest joy if I were to choose it. What is your weird and how would your life be different if you were to choose it more often?

While my experience is my own, many have similar stories of choices they made to try and fit in which were not respecting their true nature. Others may not be aware of exactly when they gave up their own truth to try to fit into the teeny, tiny box that society seems to support as normal, yet it still happens.

The greatest crime is when one chooses to withhold self loving in its many forms in hopes of accessing a resemblance of love elsewhere. This is the first step to losing oneself and the very crucial relationship with Supreme Consciousness.

"Everything you seek is within." – Swami Muktananda

The practice of yoga is meant to help us achieve many things, but the most important is the elimination of samskaras, the subtle impressions of our past actions so that we can eventually reach enlightenment or Samadhi and have direct experience of Supreme Consciousness and the oneness of all that is. The process of enlightenment however is not for wimps. It's not the airy, fairy vision that many portray. It is a highly destructive process, a complete eradication of the many lies that we believed to be true about ourselves and the universe and the breaking away of all aspects of untruth in order to unveil the Absolute Truth of all that you are and your place in the universe. Whew! That's big! The more we open and become aware of these higher truths, life in this reality can become more ease and grace. Tapping into this offers greater knowing and peace that can help support all parts of your life and living.

The ancient saints, yogis and great teachers of past and present have always understood that the state of our mind is absolutely key to our quality of life. We create our lives based on the lens through which we experience situations. Very few of us actually experience life as it is because we have so many filters (samskaras) in place that color our experience one way or another.

What would it be like to clear away those filters and experience life and the totality of all that we truly are moment to moment? How much would be available to us then if we were not shutting out major parts?

Life is a mirror. Whatever story we have running within us is projected out and we see it in everything around us. This happens all the time, but one very clear example is when I was going through a very sad time many years ago. I was moving into a new place and I remember commenting that the paint my new home looked grey and the texture on the walls looked like tears. It actually didn't look like that, but that was the state of my mind. The home was actually light and sunny and the texture was just like the walls of many other homes I had lived in, but the grief I felt inside was being mirrored back to me.

We've all seen or perhaps experienced ourselves in situations where our inner reality was different than what we were trying to portray on the outside, yet life mirrored right back to us what was happening inside.

Have you ever felt the constricted sensation of anger in your body and then observed how life around you seemed to also constrict? And on the other side, have you ever been in such a state of expansive joy that life seemed to flow with more ease and abundance? The universe reflects back to us the essence that we hold inside. Our purest essence is that of space, abundance, love and joy. So, when you choose to be in that space, you will find it more easy to connect with the wisdom of the universe.

As I have developed a better relationship with myself and my greater knowing, my life has begun to unfold with ease and joy that is sometimes quite shocking. This is not the life I used to live. It's totally new and flows with so much more ease.

What if you were to step through the mirror and leave the body and all the stories behind, like clothing. You would then experience yourself as you truly are, limitless, boundless, infinite space and potential. How can you choose that reality while you are still in the body?

"The mind is everything. What you think you become."
– Buddha

Thoughts have power! I'm sure you've heard about Masaru Emoto and his amazing experiments with the effects of words and thoughts on the formation of water crystals... clear evidence on how our thoughts affect form. Water crystals exposed to words like "Love" and "Thank you" are light and beautiful. While water crystals exposed to words like "Hate" and "War" appear dirty and ugly.

Professionals say that 70% or more of our thoughts are typically negative and take away our power. What effect does that have on our bodies and the world around us? This is why it is absolutely crucial to take command of our thoughts, especially the subconscious thoughts which will then shift all aspects of our life and living.

Becoming aware of your thoughts is the first step to taking command of your life and shifting once and for all the direction and experience of your life.

Our subconscious beliefs make up the majority of the matrix of our reality. These beliefs create a sort of comfort thermostat which defines the perceived limits we have for ourselves and our lives. Anytime we move outside of these limits, either up or down, we will scramble to get back within those limits. Once we change our belief patterns, we change this comfort thermostat and we change our lives.

The comfort thermostat works like this... Let's say your idea of success is earning between $4000 and $5000 a month. You think that if you were to reach that all your problems would be solved and life would move along just swimmingly. So, you work your butt off with that target in mind. You don't even consider anything greater because your comfort thermostat won't allow it. It's as if nothing exists for you beyond your thermostat setting. That's simply not in your current reality or awareness. Then let's say you reach your goal and things are good. In fact, they are so good that you unexpectedly begin earning much more than that. It's continues to be good for awhile, but then before you know it major problems begin to arise seemingly out of nowhere and out of your control and your money starts plummeting. What happened? You surpassed your comfort thermostat and thus self destructed in order to bring you back down into your comfort zone. This will happen over and over and over again until you reset that thermostat. People usually have no idea they have set these limits for themselves because it's the invisible belief patterns that are hidden deep in our subconscious... until we dig them up and take control of our lives. When we shift those beliefs, we have the opportunity to shift our life completely.

So, how do you do this? You begin by starting with where you are.

Begin with becoming familiar with the perceived limits of your comfort zone around everything, money, relationships, travel, your job, your health, your expression in the world and so on. Take some quality time and write down where you feel comfortable and where you begin to feel discomfort. Write down what you feel your limits are in all these areas and then make a note next to each one where you feel these impressions first became ingrained. Often times we pick these up from parent figures and other significant people in our lives and often times at periods in our lives when we are most likely to be influenced such as early childhood or during times of trauma.

Once you have a good list and a good understanding (your list and your awareness will grow and change over time with your attention), choose one area to begin working on. There are lots of methods for retraining the brain although the first and most important step is shining the light of awareness there. Neuroplasticity describes the brain's ability to diminish old neural pathways while creating new, healthier ones, therefore creating a new reality for yourself.

Some of the methods that I use to retrain my brain affecting this neuroplasticity toward the life I truly desire are Meditation, Yoga NIdra and a crazy system called Access Consciousness Bars which

I offer, but there are practitioners worldwide who can support you. Anyone can do these simple practices. You are welcome to use the free Yoga Nidra recordings on my website to get you started. http://www.Andora.Love

"I am not today who I was yesterday. I am constantly new.

Every day is a new opportunity."

I've done so much of this to release old victim patterns from past abuse that I had points where I felt really unsettled. Everything that used to help form my identity and that I once used as anchors in reality vanished (or were never really there in the first place except in my imagination) and I felt that I had nothing familiar to grasp on to. While it was very uncomfortable, that's actually a fantastic sign that big change is in process. That's the time to be as present and as patient with yourself as possible.

If this happens to you, keep breathing, stay calm and keep focusing on the life you are creating for yourself. Don't allow yourself to fall into old patterns of closing down or pushing away the change you truly desire. You are on the right path. You are creating new and healthier patterns and will soon experience a feeling of even greater calm and more abundance than before. You are building up the rich soil for your future self to grow from. It's a good sign if you feel you are in unfamiliar territory for awhile. You are creating a new map, literally... in your brain. The more you do this the easier it will be to tap into the fullness of you and abundance in your career, relationships and more will flow with greater ease.

Eliminating these negative and false belief patterns does more than change the brain. It also changes your energy in a very palpable way. It is proven that the brain and heart transmit strong electromagnetic fields which transmit information between people and other conscious beings. It is believed that this capacity for energetic information exchange between people, animals, anything really with consciousness, is an innate ability that can potentially heighten awareness and mediate empathy for others. What can that do for your business and your life?

"To thine own self be true." – Shakespeare

Owning a business will challenge you on every level and in order to be successful you must be willing to break free of your comfort zone and grow into new and uncharted territory again and again. Business ownership is not for the meek. It takes real courage, strength and vision that is far above the average Joe.

Once you eliminate the falsehoods that have kept you from living your greatest truth, you can begin to reveal your most potent contribution to yourself and the universe. What if those parts of you that you have withheld from expressing and living for all these years is your greatest gift to you and the whole planet? What if you being you is exactly what the world needs most right now? Would you be willing to be that?

As you release the imprints from past, you will find it much easier to be in the present moment where everything is available to you. You will find that Supreme Consciousness is ever present and the universe is abundant. You eventually come to a state in which you recognize that there is nothing but Spirit and this is your playground. What will you choose then?

"You can start out with nothing, and out of nothing, and out of no way, a way will be made." – Reverend Michael Bernard Beckwith

Most people are living life in a kind of dream state, not fully aware nor in the moment, but experiencing life through a lens created through past life experiences. Most people are not really experiencing life as it truly is, but through the lens, like a projector of past experience. When we go beyond this, let go and remove the imprint of past, live more in the present moment we realize that we are so much more. We are not the limited ego, but one with the entire universe. There is nothing that we cannot do.

Most live life unconsciously, never realizing that we have the ability to create the lives we desire, but it comes down to choice. What choices and daily rituals have you made that have brought you to this place in your existence now? Do you desire to continue writing the same old story with same old limitations, or would you like to rewrite your story? What is possible when we add consciousness to our life creations? How about when we decrease the charge on false beliefs letting them eventually wither away and create space for our deepest soul desires to take root? The more we choose to remove those limited beliefs the more they lose their charge and the autopilots in our mind are turned off as present moment awareness is increased. What is possible then? I'll have that! How about you?

"Realize deeply that the present moment is all
you will really ever have."
– Eckhart Tolle

In the practice of Yoga Nidra we set a sankalpam. Your sankalpam is a positive statement in present tense, as if it is already true... a soul desire or an affirmation that you wish to realize in your life. This is the seed of your transformation. To empower your sankalpam, feel your heart's deepest desire in every cell of your body as if it is already true. In order to set your sankalpam in the first place you need to be crystal clear what it is you truly desire.

"Life is short. Make it sweet." – Sri Kaleshwar

Take some quality time and write down what you wish to have in your life. This has nothing to do with anyone else, just you. What would you desire if you made zero excuses and only thought of yourself? Instead of writing down the specific house or car or whatever, you can envision that, but don't be attached. Remember, the universe is infinite and far more abundant than we could ever imagine and it speaks in energy and vibration. Don't limit yourself to the very small reality you are currently aware of. What else is possible? Invite the total abundance of the universe to smile on you. Write down the feelings. Feelings combined with clarity have real power. Write this down and keep it where you will see it daily, although don't share it with others because they may try to place their limited beliefs on you in order to keep you at their level and in their reality. Revisit these soul desires often, without the constriction of attachment or judgement and feel what you are creating in your whole body as if it is already real, because it is. Then be patient as the universe reorganizes itself to actualize your desires. Don't negate it before it has a chance to arrive. Remember, the universe is infinite and while your requests will be answered, it may show up completely different than you expect. Do not reject something because it doesn't appear as you thought it should. Instead receive it with an open heart, always expressing your gratitude and asking open questions like "What else is possible?", "How does it get better than this?" Constantly choosing and staying in the question always creates more. "What are you willing to create and receive that is completely beyond your knowing?"

To empower your sankalpam more you can integrate energy pulls. Simply envision yourself holding a transparent ball of golden light in front of you. Within that ball place that which you most desire to actualize. Feel it strongly in your entire being. Then pull the energy of the whole universe through the golden ball of light and all that you desire to actualize. Pull that universal energy through the ball, through your solar plexus (area just above your navel), out your back and swirl it around your body a few times. Then send little trickles of energy back out to the universe imbued with your deepest, heartfelt gratitude. Know that the universe is hearing and feeling you and will respond. Be patient. Do this daily for just a few minutes and be ready for miracles to become your reality.

When I chose to open my yoga studio in 2002, I knew close to nothing about business. I was moved to do something which I felt was powerful enough to change people's lives forever. I was drawn to create what I felt was the "best damn yoga studio!" and I did it. That was my sankalpam. Within a few years we were winning awards and other studios began trying to imitate what I had created. That's the best kind of compliment.

I was clear and determined with most of my felt vision and while there have been many parts that fulfill my heartfelt intention, there have been other parts that totally and utterly broke me. What up? I didn't ask for that... or did I? While I had done a lot of unwinding of the old patterns in my mind over the years, there were still many hiding under the surface that affected every aspect of my business and my life as a whole. The deepest patterns can be the hardest to uproot because those are the main ones that we used to develop our personality and our ego and as those old patterns begin to dissolve it can feel as if we are dying, because a part of us is. Whether we like it or not, that is what we feel makes us who we are. Because of that I drew in people and situations that were quite damaging. Eventually over time I discovered ways to effectively diminish the deepest samskaras and open to greater awareness and life changed dramatically. Learn how to play with the universe in a way that is fun and really contributes to you and your deepest desires. I recommend adding to your sankalpam that all life comes to you with ease, joy and grace. I assure you that your life will blossom because of it.

> "I have failed over and over and over again in my life and that is why I succeed." – Michael Jordan

Because of my many challenges earlier in life and business, there were times that I felt like a total failure even though I had helped hundreds of thousands of people and had built a comfortable life for my daughter and I, even amongst serious health challenges where I was often bed bound and had to crawl to the bathroom. (Interesting creation for myself, eh?!) The thing is, everyone who is willing to create change in the world is going to fail. You have to be willing to fall flat on your face over and over again because failure is part of growth. Don't allow fear of failure to hold you back. Just make sure you get up when life knocks you down and find new and better ways of doing things. Failure is just another opportunity for growth. It's part of the path to success. While life can be smoother and easier, it will never be completely free of challenge. Don't fool yourself. Expect the best, but be prepared for the inevitable curves in the road. Allow yourself to flow with it. Invite ease and joy in everything you do. Unexpected turns in the road do not have to be painful. Everything is choice. Ask yourself, "What's right about this?" and "How can I use this to propel myself forward into even greater success and fulfillment?" You've got this!

> "Life is either a daring adventure or nothing at all."
> – Helen Keller

Everyone has fear. What matters is what you do with it. Most often times, fear is an illusion. We are trained to it constantly in our culture. Did you know that there are only two natural fears that everyone is born with: falling and loud sounds. All else is programmed.

This makes me think of circus elephants. These sweet beings are tied to a post that is stuck in the ground from the time they are very young. They learn from very early on that they are powerless to remove the stake in the ground and roam free. Like these elephants we are being trained by our environment non-stop towards fear, but we have choice. We can choose to be aware of these constant messages and choose something different.

Our subconscious has been programmed toward fear both from media and society. That combined with past hurts and traumas can instill overriding fear that infiltrates all aspects of life and living... until we choose another path. What else can we choose to receive and be?

Fear contracts and keeps us small while excitement can feed growth and joy. What if there are times when you are not actually afraid, but you've labeled it that way for one reason or another. For example, say you've owned a business for many years, but you are ready to sell. The perfect buyer finally comes through and you realize you are about to be free to do whatever you want. You are able to create something else new and wonderful or nothing at all. It's completely up to you. You feel something powerful inside and label it as fear. Friends and family tell you it's normal to feel fear because it's such a big change for you. Your whole life and identity has been wrapped up in the business, after all. Right? Or is it excitement that you are feeling? Both are powerful, potent energies. Which feels lighter to you? Which feels like more of a contribution for the life you are creating? What can you choose that will create more for you?

Emotions that have potent vibrations like excitement, passion and joy can be your ally in creating. Combine these potent vibrations with the clarity of what you desire to create (your sankalpam) and voila! Magic happens!! Condition yourself to ask expansive questions that move you towards empowerment, joy and fulfillment. Wherever your focus goes, energy flows. Yup! You are one powerful being, for sure! Claim it!!

Choose to move away from fearful thinking and shift your focus to prosperity awareness. Begin seeing abundance everywhere and make a claim to the universe. "I'm having that." Feel it in your bones that it is already coming to you. Never fear change. Be open to change. Life is what we make it.

...and sometimes things will go "wrong". What to do then? Don't focus on fixing problems. Fix your thinking and the problems fix themselves. Be open to a new interpretation of circumstances at hand. Ask, "What is right about this?" and "What can I be aware of that will change everything?" Stay in the question and see what presents. When you ask a question you automatically change the focus and direction. How can you turn what may be the worst day of your life into the best day of your life? Everything is possible.

People who are truly successful understand the value of receiving everything, the good and the bad. Everything has value when we choose to learn from it. Could a flower ever bloom if it didn't receive the contribution of the earth, sun and rain? Does a rose fret when it begins to rain, or does it drink in the nourishment that will allow it to flower so sweetly? What contributions are you pushing away in order to fulfill the old stories you have playing? What else is possible?

> "Your task is not to seek for love, but merely to seek and find all the barriers within yourself that you have built against it." – Rumi

The essence of the universe and the essence of your soul is Love Absolute.

You are the creator of your life, every part of it, everything you see, hear, feel, experience. You want to do good, you have to feel good. When you choose to take responsibility for your life, you will notice that things flow with more ease. Here's the thing. The universe really does have your back. All you have to do is wake up and choose to ask and receive the many contributions the universe is wanting to share with you. Are you ready to receive that kind of unconditional loving? Stop sending negative prayers into the universe and instead choose positive prayers that fulfill your desires and contribute to the whole planet. How do you speak to yourself internally? What daily rituals do you regularly partake in and how are they serving you, or not serving you? Everything is energy. What can you choose differently to create the life you desire?

The world doesn't need more followers. The world needs more courageous, compassionate leaders who are aware of their potency and use that to help awaken the masses from the dream of ignorance and separation. You, my friend are an infinite being with abilities and awarenesses beyond your imagining. We've all heard stories of a mother lifting a car off her child or someone healing themselves instantly of a "terminal disease". This is only out of the ordinary because we have forgotten that this potency is our true nature. Did you know that there are saints in India and around the world who have so completely mastered their mind and their senses that they can live without food or water yet continue to achieve great miracles. These beings are called siddhas or the perfected ones. They are not different or special, they have just spent their life focus on achieving this level of awareness. We are all potent, infinite beings with these same capacities but have chosen to believe in something else. What else can we be aware of that will change everything? If we were to choose that greater awareness and totality of being, how would our lives be different?

When you choose to let go of the limiting reality which has had hold of you all your life and step into the greatness of you, your business, your relationships and all aspects of your life will flow abundantly. They are all connected. You will not be held captive by the collective unconscious of lack and separation. Instead you will find that you have unlimited access to the wisdom of the universe. What is possible then? Can you feel it?

In order to achieve this, you must be willing to step completely into a space of self loving. Our culture looks down on this one thing that could literally change everything. Can you imagine a world where everyone actually loved themselves? This goes so much deeper than the surface of love. It means to love the very essence of all that you are. The trance of separation would dissolve. Crime would be non-existent. Most people don't even know what it means to love themselves which means they don't really know what it means to love another. I absolutely believe that life on our planet would change dramatically if we all took responsibility of loving ourselves absolutely and unconditionally first. This begins with our thoughts, then translates to our words and actions.

You can start by first getting clear and then setting your sankalpam. Then spend time every day doing things that will help quiet your monkey mind and reestablish your focus on what's important to you at a soul level. Stop the negative inward talk. Listen to the small, sweet voice within you that first appears like a whisper, but the more you listen, the louder and more clear it will be. Let your vulnerability become your strength. What are those parts of you that you have held at bay, that you have spent so much energy trying to hide? Who are you really? What gift are you to the world? Be that. The world needs you to be fully you. Living small doesn't serve anyone. What energy, space and consciousness can you be every minute of every day that will be most loving to you and be the greatest contribution to the world, all at the same time? Be that! And in every moment be grateful for this life and your place in it. Gratitude and self love will nourish everything else in your life and being. This body of yours is a temple. Take care of it and it will take care of you. With this in place watch your relationships, your career, your health, your entire life blossom.

"In the end, only three things matter: how much you loved, how gently you lived and how gracefully you let go of things not meant for you." – Buddha

The Author

Andora Freedom

www.CreatingBusinessBeyondThisReality.com/andora-freedom

CHAPTER 20

Business as (Un)usual

MEGAN SILLITO

In 2013, after running a coaching and workshop business for eighteen years, I was standing one morning beside Heidi, a marketing strategist, looking at my dining room table. It was filled with pictures of all my projects, both current and planned. She asked me what I saw in all these pictures and why they were important to me. I spoke excitedly about my programs, about my ideas that I wanted to bring to fruition, and their possible impact on the world.

She listened, and then she said, "Now put your business hat on and tell me what you see. What is different?"

I was like, "Whoa, I have a business hat?" In that moment I realized I had never looked at myself as an entrepreneur or even a business owner. I knew in that instinctive way you know, that this realization was going to be a game changer for me.

Playfully, I found a hat nearby and put it on, and looked at my layout of projects. Startled, I looked again. Instantly, I saw things in my plans I had never seen before. I could understand how certain things probably wouldn't work in the order I had placed them. I also saw possibilities to open revenue streams I hadn't considered before. I realized then and there that the way I had perceived me and my business was actually a limitation of epic proportions that kept me on the hamster wheel of "time for money."

When I shared this experience with my partner who has been an accountant for entrepreneurs for over 25 years, she was surprised saying I was the quintessential entrepreneur. Then she posed the question. "If you don't see yourself as an entrepreneur, how do you see yourself?"

When I asked myself that question, I felt sick as the awareness bubbled up that I had seen myself only as a "service provider." UGH-HHHHH! No wonder I resisted creating systems that would create revenue streams that didn't involve me directly serving.

For the next several months I began asking myself questions, opening up my mind to see me and my business differently. After a about a year, I was introduced to Simone Milasas' *Joy of Business* audio book. Wow, the ideas there in blew my mind as I was taken on a journey to literally undo all my structures and beliefs about business. As it turns out, I had bought a version of business that was not mine. I'm embarrassed to say that I saw business as an "old boys" club where the likes of chaotic me was not welcome or desired. I believed business had to look linear with forms and structures and to me that felt oh so limiting and quite frankly, boring. No wonder I didn't want to see myself as a business owner and had completely gone unconscious about my genius capacities in business.

In my business, almost every day, I help people open up to who they are and to what they can do and astonishingly, I had not seen this gaping hole in my own universe. Since then, I have become aware that I have capacities around creating business and revenue streams that I didn't ever give myself credit for. For instance, a few years ago I was getting ready to launch one of my signature programs, Play

Your Way to Money and my partner kept wondering why I wasn't "doing" anything to enroll and launch the program as the starting date loomed closer. I told her that I hadn't felt the thread yet, and when I did it would happen. I was really grateful for her question, which had me ask myself, how was I creating it? I didn't sense I was procrastinating so I looked deeper to see what was happening. The next morning I asked the question of the universe. Show me how I create? It was one of the most life changing questions I've ever asked myself. (But please don't ask yourself this; it may just rock your world!) I realized I was energetically creating and enrolling for the program before the physical aspects fell into place. My tendency is to follow a thread, do a bit of this and that, and then POW!! I'm in the deep end of creation. Within 48 hours I had grasped the context and completely filled the program.

I used to discount the way I created calling it procrastination or flying by the seat of my pants but actually I create things organically and energetically so that when it's time for physical action there's a whole mass of energy behind the action that speeds up the actualization in a way that looks like magic or luck to the outside world. Heidi, the marketing strategist has said many times to me in jest and seriousness, "You defy me and the laws of marketing." I'm continually curious about new ways people looking for me may find me, or what I can offer or discover that offers genuine benefit to others. I follow the energy and discover and create systems that are simple and work for me. Instead of fighting the systems that feel inauthentic or pushy to me, I look for new ways that feel fun and easy.

I get ideas that are unusual and quirky and are just zany enough to work most of the time, and its ok when it doesn't work because it generally teaches me something new about what I need for the next time. I sense futures that are not yet visible. As an instigator, I'm generally ahead of the curve and am learning to nurture and play with my ideas in a new way, looking for new ways to find the seekers who are on the edge looking for the next evolution of transformation and creation. My weird way of doing business and telling people that they can be successful doing it their weird way is what I'm excitedly bringing forward today. And I give myself permission to keep creating on the edge.

HAVE YOU BEEN IN MY SHOES?

Have you judged yourself as lacking when the truth is, you were never meant to follow the status quo? Are you an esoteric or spiritual being who doesn't think you can create a viable business because the way you create is so different than anything you see in the world? Have you judged yourself as inconsistent or a procrastinator? What if you have massive capacities in the areas you define as your weakness, capacities that are actually beyond what most people can access? Let me be the "town crier" who runs through the streets telling you and everyone like you; "You can make a successful business doing what you love, creating in a way that is uniquely you."

WHAT'S YOUR BLUEPRINT?

The truth is that it's imperative that those of us who hold the blueprints (That's you, silly!) For a new reality choose to be and do whatever is required to actualize our world changing visions. Have you ever thought that because your projects are incredibly unique, the way those will be created will be unusual as well? What do you know about creating business that no one on this planet has a clue about? What if we stopped buying into the 5- step marketing structures and followed the consciousness and energy of our creations using our singular awareness to create beyond what we have seen everyone else do? What if we stopped comparing ourselves to people who are creating usual products and services in usual ways? What would be possible if we weirdos (the original definition of weird meant to harness ones supernatural powers and elements to create ones destiny) brought our different and wild ideas to fruition in ways that changed the world and generated perpetual and increasing wealth?

Consider the possibility that you may have something the universe requires and if you don't choose to bring it forward in a tangible visible way, the world will not have it.

WHAT DOES IT TAKE?

So what does it take to create a business that feels like it is being created from who we truly are, through giving the gifts we most desire to give? Funnily enough, I can't answer that for you because how you create is as individual to you as your fingerprint. However, What I can do is point you in a direction; a way to look for that creator code in you that will allow you to catch the wave of your creation. P.S. Your wave will likely not look like those around you.

The first step is, you must forgive yourself for not being able to create like everyone else! If you're like me and have had a deep desire to bring yourself and your talents to the world, you might have paid for a few dozen business and/or marketing courses and failed miserably. (Of course you did.) So what if you're a "Franklin Covey" drop out, or quit "The Best 7 Steps to 6 Figures in 9 Months" after week 3? The people who are successful in those programs actually create better in linearity, structures and systems. And the good news is that's not how YOU create. What if YOU are already beyond that? Stay with me here.

One of my mentors, Dain Heer, says that when we don't see and acknowledge the miracles we are and the miracles we create we will basically undo them or create the opposite. By telling myself I was "bad" at business and marketing, I was not only denying my potencies but I was energetically putting up blocks to people engaging with my products and material. I was also unable to discover or see the channels that would allow me to successfully bring my ideas to fruition, lead the market place, and capitalize when the wave hit. So, what if you're doing a similar thing in your world? And what if your capacity for business is beyond what you ever thought possible?

START ASKING QUESTIONS

After you've forgiven yourself for being a weirdo, you might want to start asking what capacities you have in business and marketing that are beyond what you have ever considered. As you get awareness from this questioning you must begin to acknowledge the brilliance of you. There is a quote from a sermon of Christ (in the Gospel of Thomas from the Apocrypha) which states "If you bring forth that which is in you it will save you, if you do not it will destroy you." You must be willing to see what is truly great in you. As you do that, you will also be aware of the pieces that you need from other people, other talents to support your creation. I'm not sure all the reasons we fight so vehemently against our greatness, but I do know if you desire to make the difference you know inside you came here to do, you must say YES to the capacities you have been denying and hiding from you and the world. You must truly see who you are.

To assist you in that awareness, I have a few specific questions and statements you can begin to use to open up new possibilities for you, your projects and business.

1. What capacities do I have (in marketing) that I've been refusing to acknowledge that if I did, and turned them up, would generate a result beyond what I have never imagined?

2. What (entrepreneurial) capacities do I have that are unlike anything I have ever seen?

3. Body, show me the way I create best. Show me my creator codes.

4. "What potency of (business or...) am I refusing that if I would choose it would open me up to the greatness I've been hiding from me?

5. Every time I hear myself say "I'm not good at...." I simply ask this question and listen and follow the energy.

As you play with these questions you will begin to have awareness of what some of these capacities are. Some will have names and some will simply be energies that but you will be able to sense them and acknowledge them. These are questions and statements you could continue to ask for the rest of your life, as the brilliance of who we are and what we can do is absolutely infinite.

JUST SHOW UP

One of the biggest reasons we all pretend we're not good at something is because we don't want to know how truly potent we are. In truth, we're more afraid of our greatness then our weaknesses. And yet, if there is one secret to creating an awesome life and business it's this; we must choose to show up.

I find that people often sit on the sidelines assuming everyone else has some secret code that they don't. And they don't launch anything until they've figured out the secret code! We're all scared and insecure it's just that some of us are scared and choose to show up any way, warts and all. My virtual assistant delighted me the other day stating that in working for me she had surprisingly discovered that I don't have my "ducks in a row" even though I'm a successful coach.

I've created a great living for over two decades changing people's lives and doing what I love. And I've done it simply by showing up. I'm willing to show up and figure it out as I go. I'm willing to be scared and not prepared and show up anyways. I'm willing to not be an expert and be a work in progress. Every day I have a choice to show up. Now I'm willing to show up; now, I know how.

WHAT DOES IT TAKE TO SHOW UP

Business isn't science it's an experiment, a venture into the unknown. Showing up in your business could look like taking a nap, asking a question, feeling rejected, or pulling an all-nighter launching a project. So, how do you know? Ask a question. Be willing to ask your business. Be willing to be surprised. Magic in business doesn't live in the ordered structures of predefined outcomes it lives in the chaos of pure creation.

Study and hone your craft every day. Continued and constant effort is essential. I'm fascinated with learning ways to improve and expand who I am and what I'm creating in the world. I'm obsessed with creating a life that other people would desire. Be in the process of always creating a greater version of your dreams and you will not only have the life you want but you will be irresistible to your perspective clients and customers.

One of the first things I say to coaches who come to me to help them launch their businesses is to first design a life they would pay to learn how to get. When people invest in themselves through you and your business, they are actually buying your energy and your vibration.

When I look for a healer I look for someone who has a vibrancy that I would like to have. (It always surprises me how many healers are wounded). When I invest in mentors, I love learning business from people who are creating impact and wealth while having a damn good time.

To show up in the biggest way possible, you must realize there is only one of you. Your clients/customers are literally looking for a vibration or an energy that they don't have words for. If you are not being that vibration, and living that, your customers will have a difficult time finding you. We weirdos don't necessarily fit into the current mold of business entrepreneurs but we are gifted entrepreneurs and creators and as we discover who we are, show up, and continue to choose we will create things this world has never dreamt of.

Since putting on my business cap on four years ago so much is different. Now that I'm an entrepreneur instead of a "service provider" I wake up to unexpected money in my bank account because I have ways for people to find me and to connect to my products and services that don't involve me showing up at a particular time and space. When an idea comes I ask how I can create it, who is meant to help actualize it, and what systems want to be instituted instead of feeling like I don't know how. I did a simple last minute launch before coming to Noosa Australia, where I am writing this chapter from, where I created and generated 2k in a few days. These things are happening because I'm honoring my capacities and the different ways I create. The best part is I'm just getting started. I can't wait to see what else I can dream up.

IS IT TIME TO JUMP IN?

One of my greatest joys these days is inspiring people to discover how they truly create and liberating the genius creator in them. I've made a living creating programs and services that I wished someone had offered me that I couldn't find anywhere else. I love being a space of "Do it your way." You have capacities in business you've never dreamed of. If you look at almost everyone you truly admire, you admire him or her because no one was being that or creating that before they did. What is it you are here to create that no one has ever seen or been? Is now the time to unleash them? Would you be willing to be weird and create like no one else? Would you be willing to not be ready and start anyway? What do you know that you have never been willing to know that if you would allow yourself to know it would generate a business and life you never imagined possible? One last thing, there are others out there doing it their way, being as weird as they can be, and creating wealth on every level. This book is filled with them. JUMP IN!

The Author

Megan Sillito
www.CreatingBusinessBeyondThisReality.com/megan-sillito

CHAPTER 21

Kindness Builds an Empire

Erica Glessing

She was so frustrated. She had done "everything."

She still could not "do what she loved," and had to muck about in a day job that she could not stand.

Her healing and consciousness workshop business was beaten up and bruised from years of her neglect and downright disappointment.

So, when we met, we started with a conversation. I heard her say for over a year that she couldn't make her business work, and she was about to give up.

These were the kinds of messages she was saying to the energy of her business daily:

- You aren't good enough

- You aren't performing well enough

- If you could only support me I could leave the job I hate

- You are never going to make it

- You aren't worth my time because it never works out

It always amazes me the ease with which people can slip into a boot camp sort of mentality with their business, where they are ready to change everything, without realizing that in speaking with disappointment, disdain, dislike, and discouragement, the outcomes are not likely to be shiny and bright. It's easier to build an empire when you speak to your business with a curiosity and genuine adoration.

As we looked into the characteristics of her business, I saw something beautiful tucked inside the beaten down places where she had been bad-mouthing the results for so long. I saw a glimpse of possibility that with nourishment could grow.

I began to speak to that glimpse of possibility, and so did she. She intuitively grasped the entire world of her relationship with her business in those few minutes. Everything changed after that day, for her business.

You can liken your business to a child, if you like. Does a child do better when he or she is yelled at, berated, criticized, and told that she is not enough? Or when she is shown new pathways for success and encouraged when she makes milestones or grows and changes?

En route to building your empire, see if you can expand the vision for the business to be as large as it would like to be. See if you can trust that you will guide it with ease, with grace, and with a knowing that is enjoyable. Yes, it is infinitely possible to enjoy growing your business. Even if it does not quite seem like an empire, yet.

Obstacles

The sneaky thing about this conversation with business is that if you don't take time to truly look at what you are saying (with and without words), you might have a challenge changing it. So, take time to review the words you use when describing your business to others. And then be sure to look beyond this at how you are showing up to others, and the telepathic "energy" of your business that you are sharing (even possibly without full awareness) to others when you speak about your business.

I had a wildly successful summer one year, inviting people into someone else's business (we will just call it a multi-level marketing business for the fun of it). When I looked back at that flash of success, I saw that I was sharing the absolute concrete opportunity to succeed with my messaging, and it did not require a script. It was just me sharing "this works," and everyone who joined that summer enjoyed how well it worked.

The Commitment to Your Empire

When you stand in greatness, you stop giving up after one try. What if you chose to graduate from high school, but after two months of kindergarten you were not able to pass the 12th grade exam for high school graduation?

Or, what if you desired to speak Spanish, and after two hours of instruction, you could not do it fluently?

Building an empire is going to require whatever it requires. Think back to math, if you studied math in school. Maybe your neighbor required four hours to do her homework, and it took you seven minutes. You cannot "know" what it will take to build your empire, your way, in sync with your vision, in keeping with your desires, until you step in and start.

I will share the first time I did a #1 bestseller campaign for a group book, we made it to #6000 ranking on Amazon. Books start about 18 million ranking, so that is an awesome day to go up to #6000.

Now I can collaboratively work with authors to bring a #1 ranking.

Then, I couldn't yet. Couldn't yet did not mean give up.

That's the message I'd like to share most: don't give up. Keep seeing new ways and new connections, and asking new questions.

"Business, what do you require of me today?"

"Business, what can I bring today to exceed all of my expectations with grace?"

As you ask questions, then follow what shows up and keep asking for more.

That, for me, is the happiness I find in building my empire. It is the way I am always uncovering new ways to grow the business! I wonder what this next year will bring? I'm always insatiably curious!

"Creation is inherent in everything you do. Make something today!" ~ Poet Ntozake Shange

THE END

The Author

Erica Glessing

www.CreatingBusinessBeyondThisReality.com/erica-glessing

CPSIA information can be obtained
at www.ICGtesting.com
Printed in the USA
FFHW022229271118
49657808-54033FF